A MOUSE IN THE MANSE

LAVINIA DERWENT

A Mouse in the Manse

Illustrated by Elizabeth Haines

Hutchinson
London Melbourne Sydney Auckland Johannesburg

Hutchinson & Co (Publishers) Ltd

An imprint of Century Hutchinson Ltd

17–21 Conway Street, London W1P 6JD

Hutchinson Publishing Group (Australia) Pty Ltd
16–22 Church Street, Hawthorn, Melbourne,
Victoria 3122, Australia

Hutchinson Group (NZ) Ltd
32–34 View Road, PO Box 40–086, Glenfield, Auckland 10

Hutchinson Group (SA) Pty Ltd
PO Box 337, Bergvlei 2012, South Africa

First published 1985

© Lavinia Derwent 1985

Set in Bembo by
The Castlefield Press, Moulton, Northampton

Printed and bound in Great Britain by
Anchor Brendon Ltd, Tiptree, Essex

ISBN 0 09 162070 8

Contents

1. The Borders are Best

'If I should die before I wake . . .'

Every night I breathed the childhood prayer before laying me down to sleep, and sighed with relief in the morning when I found I was still alive.

'Oh good! I'm still here!'

But it took a long time to gather my senses. That morning I lay half-bemused, straining my ears for the familiar farmyard sounds: cocks crowing, cows mooing, workhorses clumping, pails rattling, the shepherd whistling to his collies, and in the kitchen Jessie's clogs clattering on the floor.

Comforting homely sounds, the prelude to another carefree day. Freedom to roam all over the farm, to climb trees, hunt for eggs, swing on gates, help Jock-the-herd with the sheep, run barefoot to my ruined castle on the hill. I could sit for ages on the crumbling battlements, reading and writing, or just gazing at the view: the Eildons on one side, the Cheviots on the other, with that foreign country – England – just over the horizon. The Borders were best!

But as I turned on my pillow I could not hear any of the sounds, or smell a whiff of manure in the morning air. Then I remembered, and jolted myself wide awake!

This was not my small skylit bedroom at home in the farmhouse. It was larger, less cosy, and looked out on a backgreen where the washing hung.

The washing! Mercy! Had I forgotten to bring it in last night? I hoped the minister's underpants and my skimpy petticoat had not fallen off. Otherwise, Bush, our frisky puppy, would have carried them off to deposit on a nearby doorstep. Our neighbours were well acquainted with the Manse underwear, forever bringing back grubby singlets and night-gowns.

The Manse!

I sprang out of bed, realizing there would be no carefree day ahead of me; no running wild, no reading or writing, no moment to call my own. Above all, no Jessie in the kitchen to stir the porridge and give me the benefit of her cold commonsense. *Rummlegumption,* she called it.

Jessie loomed larger in my mind than my parents when I thought of home. She had always been there, helping in the house when not working as a bondager in the fields, and giving me the benefit of her no-nonsense philosophy. She was the shepherd's sister, a staunch, upright, *hard* character, yet with a softer centre which she sometimes revealed to me when I was a child. When my parents were too busy, she found time to listen to me and help me over many a hump. Jessie was my life-line.

Her sayings I thought better than the Bible's. 'The back's aye made for the burden,' she had assured me when I left the shelter of the farmhouse to become a Lady of the Manse; but it was a heavy burden for such a young lassie more accustomed to climbing trees than presiding over the Women's Guild. And it was not easy to remember my p's and q's all the time. (To be *perjink,* Jessie called it.) Thank goodness! it was not to be a life-sentence. I was only a stop-gap till my bachelor brother looked around and found a proper lady to fill my place.

Hurry up, H.J.!

His name was Henry John but he was known as H.J. in the family (and still Sonny to his mother) and, though older and wiser than I, he too had a lot to learn in this his first charge. He had thrown himself heart and soul into it and was a great success with the parishioners, particularly the young folk who had been accustomed to older, staider ministers. (I had to think of him now, not as my brother, but as 'the minister'.) H.J. would often discard his dog-collar, leap fences, run races, organize sports' days, and generally behave like a human being. He was a new breed, determined to take the stuffiness out of religion without shocking the more orthodox members of the congregation.

We had both carried our burdens for over a year and some of my rough corners had been smoothed out. I was beginning to know the parishioners as real people and to be less tongue-tied when I had to address a meeting. But oh! It was a cruel change from the rough-and-tumble life I had led at home. I dared not scramble over dykes, appear in public with wrinkled stockings, *run* down the street or do a hop-skip-and-jump if I felt like it. Ladies of the Manse had to keep their brakes on.

But it was a bonus to be still in the Borders – in Berwickshire – and still on a frontier with England; though it was a very different county from Roxburghshire where I had been brought up. Flatter and more featureless. I missed the hills; but the folk were kindly and had begun to accept me in spite of my inadequacies. And I was pleased to hear so many compliments about H.J. 'My! Isn't the minister nice? He's so *human!*' But now and again I heard one about myself, which lightened my load. 'The minister's sister's not bad!'

Not good, however, at running this big barren Manse. *Running* was the right word. When out of sight of the parishioners I forgot to be sedate and almost galloped. For the Manse had been built to accommodate a large family, with huge draughty rooms and long passages where I scuttled the hundred yards when summoned by the doorbell. At least I got plenty of exercise.

It was a constant battle against time, trying to be in three places at once: the front door, the back door, and at the kitchen stove. The stove itself was a spiteful beast which either roared like a furnace or died of neglect the moment my back was turned. Worst of all was the temperamental water-supply which had to be coaxed in trickles from the tap. When it stopped altogether I had to start pumping. Up-down!

Up-down! How often I kicked that pump in passing and got nothing but a sore toe for my pains!

But that was only in the house. A Lady of the Manse was expected to undertake many parish duties as I soon found out from Mrs Sturrock, the chief elder's wife, a big bossy woman who liked laying down the law and thought she had found a soft mark in me. 'Oh! You'll soon find something to do!' she assured me when I first arrived, as if I would otherwise be sitting twiddling my thumbs. I paled with apprehension when she reeled off some of the treats in store for me: running the Guild, visiting the sick, taking a Bible class, joining a sewing-bee, organizing the Brownies. But by now I was beginning to get her measure, and Mrs Sturrock was learning that even a Manse worm could occasionally turn and say 'No!' Even so, my thumbs remained un-twiddled.

It was the constant stream of visitors that left me breathless, all expecting cups of tea, if not full meals, and sometimes overnight accommodation. A Manse was an ever-open door so, even though we might be on short commons ourselves, meals had somehow to be conjured up, beds made ready, and at least one room had to be tidy enough for unexpected visitors. 'Come in!' I said to all and sundry before scampering back to the kitchen. 'I'll run and put the kettle on.'

It was a great change for me to see so many strangers at the door, for at the farmhouse we had no unexpected callers and no passers-by since the farm road led nowhere except to the hills. It was only an odd tramp who found his way to the farmstead, and even to gaze at the wrinkles on his begrimed face

13

was a wonder to me. Now, I had too many wonders, too many strange faces, and not enough time to examine each minute detail.

I was always behind, like the cow's tail, and forever on the look-out for time-saving dodges. So that morning, when I came to my senses, I decided to descend the stairs by the quickest method. As I slid down the banisters at top speed, I hoped to hear some sound of activity from the kitchen. Not, alas, Jessie calling out: 'Come on, lassie! The porridge is ready,' but Nettie dumping a pan into the sink. She was better than nothing.

Nettie (Oor Net) was my daily help, one of a large family of Hoggs who lived in a tumbledown cottage up the Loaning, a rough track beyond the Manse. She had not long left school and was raw, like myself, but good-natured and willing. So we put up with each other and got on a treat, the blind leading the blind. I never tried to 'improve' her, though occasionally I winced when she came out with an un-Manse-like expletive. 'Holy Moses!' was her favourite which she used so frequently it was infiltrating into my own vocabulary. Many a time I had to swallow it, especially when confronting Mrs Sturrock.

I had sympathy with Oor Net when I saw her gazing wistfully out of the window across to the school playground where she had recently romped with her friends. I turned a blind eye when she occasionally took French leave to join them and their skipping-ropes. For two pins I would have downed tools and joined them myself. But no! I was a Lady of the Manse!

Nettie's small brother, Wee Wullie, was my special favourite. He ran errands, took Bush for walks, posted letters, and hung on the minister's words. H.J. was God to Wee Wullie.

God was teaching him to play the fiddle, a painful process to those listening, though the laddie had an ear for music and was taking it seriously. 'I canna let Him doon,' he declared, fiddling away like mad.

'Was that the Blue Danube?' I asked him one day, after hearing him going over a piece dozens of times.

'I dinna ken,' said Wee Wullie. 'It just came oot ma heid.' So maybe we had a future composer in our midst.

When a family emergency arose, and there were many, the Hoggs' chubby baby was brought to the Manse and dumped on the bed in the small servant's room off the kitchen, where he lay kicking his legs and bawling for attention. He was the first baby H.J.

had christened and had the privilege of taking the minister's name. So Henry John Hogg was practically one of our relations. By now he was beginning to crawl and to pull himself on to his feet. I hoped he would be a slow developer, otherwise he would soon be pulling things off the table.

One way and another the Manse could scarcely be called a settled household. As I neared the kitchen door that morning I heard an ominous sound. The latest addition to the household was in residence. At home I had been accustomed to livestock wandering in and out of the open door, but that was a farmhouse. This was a Manse – no place for a pet lamb.

It was Nettie's pet lamb and – like Mary's – it followed her one day down the Loaning and refused to go back.

'Damnation!' exclaimed Oor Net, defeated. The pet lamb had pushed its way through her legs and into the kitchen. 'Holy Moses! I'll never get him oot!'

I tried hard to put my foot down and shoo the beast away, but Baa-Baa would not be persuaded to leave once he was in residence. (He had to be called something, so I christened him Baa-Baa on the spur of the moment.) He and Bush had a boxing-match to begin with, then suddenly declared a truce and lay on the kitchen rug together. But as he had a habit of leaving his mark behind and we often had to clear up his droppings in a hurry, he was not our most welcome guest.

The greatest problem was keeping Baa-Baa out of the minister's way. H.J. frequently fell over the lamb and roared: 'Blast!' in a voice of thunder. Often he threatened to wring the beast's neck and nearly carried out his threat one day when Baa-Baa got into his study, knocked over his music-stand and scattered sermon-paper in all directions, before leaving his calling-card on the rug. After that H.J. kept a niblick at the ready and was often to be seen pursuing the lamb with the intent of doing him bodily harm.

Nettie and I were adept at covering up his tracks and telling tarradiddles to save Baa-Baa's skin – and ours – from the wrath of the minister who was not, however, as hard-hearted as all that. For one day I keeked into the study and found His Reverence trying out his sermon on the lamb, sitting placidly at his feet looking up at him as if understanding every word. Now and again H.J. got up and paced back and forth, stepping over Baa-Baa and stooping to give him a pat in passing. It was almost a Biblical scene.

Ours was not an organized household. Oh dear no! I often wondered what the previous incumbents, pillars of righteousness, would have thought of our higgledy-piggledy ways. Perhaps it would have surprised them to see the kirk so well-filled on Sundays, in spite of the new minister's unorthodox behaviour.

They might even have conceded that *I* was trying. For I did try to do my duties though I was never sure what they were. But I was certain-sure of one thing. They were unpaid.

My brother had been trained for the job and received a pittance of a stipend from which he doled out a meagre amount to cover the household expenses; every coin had to be accounted for and there was never a mite left for personal items. My parents

17

occasionally came to the rescue if I had to buy a new coat or a pair of shoes, for I had to look 'decent'; but, since I was being housed and fed, it never occurred to them to give me an allowance for smaller items. What about toothpaste, darning-wool, replacements for broken teapots or cups? (Oor Net was a smasher.) And what happened if my hot-water-bottle burst? I just did without.

I tried to augment my private purse by scribbling 'pieces' for the newspapers, which brought in ten-and-sixpence here and – oh joy! – a guinea there, and I had hopes of writing a book some day. There were plenty of characters around to put in it; but och! there was never time. It was more important to think what to give the minister for his supper.

Sometimes when I played hooky to give Bush a quick walk in the gloaming I met Aileen, the gentle sickly daughter of one of the gentry, slowly exercising her own dog, Jasper. We paused to exchange 'literary' talk for she, too, was attempting to write and we had become friends when we discovered our mutual interest. We inspired each other and I could not help envying her having the whole day in which to polish a sentence, and no worries about meals which would appear as if by magic, served with gleaming silver accoutrements. She did not even know the names of some of the servants. Yet, I forgot my envy when I saw how slowly she walked and how frequently she had to stop and struggle for breath.

One night I stopped, too, and said in a puzzled voice, 'Help! What on earth can I make for supper?'

Aileen was more puzzled than I. 'Let me think. What about pheasant or salmon? Or perhaps venison? That's rather nice . . .'

'Och! Never heed! I'll do something with sausages. Must run!'

Our conversations always ended with my leaving her in mid-sentence and racing Bush back home.

H.J. had a good appetite and it was no compliment to my cooking that he ate so heartily when we were invited out for meals, especially to the big houses where, indeed, pheasant and venison were likely to be on the menu. On such occasions my own appetite vanished – I was so busy watching and listening to the strange breed of folk round the table. Often I found myself stuffing plain bread into my mouth in the kitchen when I got home. So why hadn't I accepted another helping of salmon when I got the chance, as H.J. had done?

Oh! but I was being fed with better things. I tucked them away at the back of my head, and maybe I would bring them out some day when I got time to write that book.

2. Conversazione

'That's it!' cried my brother, knocking the top off his boiled egg.

I took no notice of him, though the egg looked shattered. For some time he had been staring into space, trying to solve one of the world's great mysteries or perhaps pondering over his sermon.

Now that he had reached a satisfactory conclusion, he got busy with his bone egg-spoon and attacked his breakfast with a good appetite.

'A conversazione,' he muttered, buttering his toast.

'What's that?' I asked in an off-hand way, pouring out his tea.

'A conversazione? It's a kind of musical evening with conversation in between. That'll do the trick.'

'What for?'

H.J. looked across at me as if I was a loony. He assumed I should read his mind and always be tuned in to his wave-length.

'For the gentry, of course!' he said impatiently. 'It's high time we returned their hospitality.'

Yes, yes! Now I saw the light. More than high time!

For ages I had hidden my head in the sand, hoping the day of reckoning would never come. We were constantly being invited to the big houses in the district for tea, supper, tennis-parties and 'Do drop in for a glass of sherry.' I knew we ought to return the compliment but how to entertain the gentry was a puzzle too difficult to solve. I had pushed it under the carpet along with other problems.

Mother, who knew what was what, was always on about it. 'You'll have to entertain those folk. It's not etiquette . . .' Oh! etiquette!

I could not picture myself showing the Major's wife round the Manse garden, she who prided herself on her own perfect grounds and could tell the pedigree of every plant along with its Latin name. What could I say? 'Here's a nice clump of nettles, and that's the minister's slipper lying on the lawn . . .'

And what could we offer inside the shabby Manse to match up to their splendours? True, they were not ostentatious; they just took gracious living for granted and were accustomed to silver cutlery and fine china, not to cracked cups and saucers that did not match.

And what could I give them to eat? 'Don't think about it,' I kept telling myself, 'and maybe it'll go away.'

But now that H.J. had grasped the nettle, I would be forced to do more than think about it. All very well for him! Having made his decision, he considered the matter settled. It would all happen as if by magic.

'Hold on!' I cried, completely put off my breakfast. 'Who are we going to invite?'

'Oh! just the gentry,' said the minister airily. He tapped them out with his egg-spoon. 'Sir Joseph and Lady Victoria, with Aileen if she's well enough to come. The Major and his wife. The Colonel and *his* wife. And I suppose we'd better ask old Miss Calder . . .'

He wrinkled his brow in distaste. Old Miss Calder who lived in a rambling house in the Loaning was our nearest neighbour and a continual irritation to us, with her smelly pug-dog, her constant complaints, her intrusions into our privacy, and her certainty that she was a cut above us intellectually. But if it was blue blood we were after she could not be excluded for, as she frequently told us, she exchanged Christmas cards with 'the Palace'!

What a gathering! With luck, I might be smitten with leprosy before the awful event.

'We'd better get up some new pieces to play,' said H.J., rising from the table and getting ready to escape to the study. 'And you'll have to put in a bit of practice with the accompaniments.'

Goodbye to my boiled egg!

When I broke the news to Oor Net she gasped: 'Holy God! I'll need to get a new peenie.'

A peenie was a pinafore, and Nettie's was a nondescript garment which she sometimes wore inside-out. And what about a little cap to go with it? We

22

went the length of making one but, no matter how hard I tried to anchor it on, it kept falling off Nettie's bushy locks till I thought I would be forced to hammer it in.

'An' what aboot curtseying?' she wanted to know. Nettie had a great respect for the gentry and obviously expected them to arrive wearing tiaras, if not crowns. (And how they would keep *them* on their heads was their own business.)

'Och! we'll think about that later,' said I, trying to put off the evil day; but later was *now*. No more time to be an ostrich, so I had to pull my thoughts together. What should I think of first? Food, drink, cutlery? How to spruce up the Manse, what to wear as a hostess, how on earth to keep Miss Calder from dominating the conversation? Playing the piano? *One-two-three-thump!*

I tackled the food first and came to some sort of conclusion. We would have a buffet. (A *boofy* Oor Net called it.) After a musical interlude in the drawing-room the visitors would descend and help themselves from the dining-room table. I had the menu in my head but it changed from day to day. Soup to begin with? Maybe! Home-cured ham from the farm? A *real* trifle, copying the kind Mother made. Perhaps an apple-tart? Cheese and biscuits. What more could they want? Like it or lump it.

'Oh Lord! I wish I was deid!' groaned Oor Net at intervals. 'I'm comin' oot in plooks.' (*Plooks* were spots, and Nettie's were always coming and going.)

But I could see she was enjoying all the stir. So was Mother. She unearthed the family silver from the farmhouse and she and Father brought it triumphantly to the Manse in the motor, along with the epergne for the centre of the table and a stiffly starched tablecloth with matching napkins.

'Let them see you know how to do things properly. And for goodness' sake, don't forget the sugar-tongs . . .'

Oh!

The news had leaked out around the village and the gossips were agog, especially Mrs Sturrock who was angling for an invitation.

'I hear you're having quite a spree,' she said, buttonholing me in the street one day.

'Oh no! just returning hospitality,' I said airily.

'Well, if there's anything I can do, I'm only too willing,' she said hopefully. 'Anything at all!'

'No thanks, Mrs Sturrock. You're very kind, but I'll manage.' (The back's aye made for the burden!)

But my back was often at breaking-point, particularly when old Miss Calder called at inconvenient moments to give me advice. I said 'Yes-yes!' to everything, meaning 'No-no!'. Finally, my patience gave out when she offered to lend me a chair. 'NO! We've got chairs,' I snapped, rounding on her.

Ah! Miss Calder informed me in her superior way, this was not an ordinary chair. It was an heirloom on which royalty had once reclined. She wouldn't lend it to everyone but Lady Victoria had a weak back and wouldn't it add a tone to our drawing-room to have *one* decent bit of furniture on view? 'NO!' I said firmly, having seen the moth-eaten chair which I suspected would disintegrate the moment anyone sat on it. 'Lady Victoria can recline on the sofa. It's nice and soggy, the very thing for a sore back.'

My back felt better after that, though Miss Calder

took a dimmer view of me than ever.

On the day of the great event H.J. suddenly became flustered and, while I was getting the table ready, tried to inveigle me into having another rehearsal of his 'pieces'. 'Just you fiddle away and I'll catch up somehow,' I told him, not with much hope.

I had too many other things on my mind, and was ageing rapidly as I attended to such tricky tasks as the beating-up of cream for the trifle (which refused to set) and filling the epergne with flowers. It looked nice enough till it turned turtle in the middle of the table, causing Oor Net to ejaculate: 'Michty God! is that no' the last straw?'

No! There were sheaves of straws to come. Mother made matters worse by ringing up at frequent intervals to give me last-ditch instructions, till I had to plead: '*Please* get off the line! I'm getting on fine. Everything's under control.' What a thumper!

Miss Calder arrived first and far too early. Oor Net, holding on to her cap with one hand, bobbed her a curtsey and gulped, 'Oh hullo! Miss Calder. Excuse the duster. We're no' quite feenished yet.'

Miss Calder looked down her nose at Nettie and sailed upstairs to the drawing-room where she sat in solitary splendour on the sagging sofa till the others arrived. H.J. was searching for his shoes as usual, and I was hastily cobbling a rent in my good frock. In my excitement, I almost forgot to breathe.

They all arrived on the doorstep together, all in evening-dress, the ladies carrying little fancy bags and all talking politely about the weather. I noticed that Lady Victoria had twinkling little buttons on her pointed shoes (or were they jewels?) and the Major's wife was wearing a cape which made her look like an outsized teddy-bear. Aileen was there, pale as a ghost. But no more ghostly than I felt. 'Breathe!' I told myself. 'It's begun, so it'll soon be past!'

They were too well-bred to pass any remarks about the Manse. If they noticed the faded wallpaper they did not comment on it, but stood in a group by the fireplace, talking amiably to Miss Calder, till the unpredictable Colonel, looking wildly around, suddenly cried: 'Charge!' and deposited himself in the largest easy-chair.

When we were all seated, Nettie arrived with a tray of drinks, and bobbed to everyone till I was sure · she would spill the sherry. Now and again I exchanged a glance with Aileen. I could tell she was taking everything in, and wondered if she would write about it later.

Later! The ordeal would be over by then.

'Let's have some music,' said my brother, taking up his fiddle.

Lady Victoria, who was in the midst of a long story, nodded her head. 'Music! Yes, that would be lovely,' she said, and continued her tale without losing the thread. H.J. waited patiently to see if she would stop, then rapped his bow on the piano for me to start. *One-two-three-thump!* We launched into our first piece, conscious of the chatter in the background.

I could scarcely see the notes on the music-sheet for straining my ears to listen to her Ladyship's account of a visit to London and Miss Calder's sycophantic replies. The others joined in the conver-

26

sation at intervals, and H.J. played louder as the hubbub increased. It was terrible!

The Colonel put his hands to his ears and wandered out to sit on the stairs. Was it the gossip or the music that had driven him away? I was never sure if the Colonel was as dotty as he pretended to be; he got out of so many tight corners by appearing to be absent-minded. How I longed to join him!

One-two-three-thump! Faster and louder! We tried to press on. H.J. would have persisted, but I realized we had reached the point of no return. What was the use of going on if no one was listening? Was it inspiration or desperation that suddenly came over me? To H.J.'s amazement – and mine – I abandoned 'Für Elise' and banged on the piano to attract attention. *Bang-bang!*

There was a frightening silence. Even Miss Calder swallowed Wordsworth's quotation about London bridge with which she hoped to impress the company, and stared at me incredulously. 'Go on!' I urged myself, though my knees were trembling. 'You can't stop now!'

So I swirled round on the music-stool and blurted out: 'Let's have a sing-song. You can all join in. What's your favourite, Major?'

I had seen him eyeing *The Students' Song Book* lying on top of the piano, and felt he was itching to renew acquaintance with old friends. 'It's here!' he cried, rising at once and flicking over the pages till he came to 'The Bonnie Banks o' Loch Lomond'. I thumped out the accompaniment, the Major took up the tune, and before long they were all joining in. Even the Colonel left his seat on the stairs and put in an occasional '*Pom-pom!*'

It had all happened so suddenly I thought I must have gone off my head. But, once started, there was no stopping them. What could H.J. do but lay aside his fiddle and join in? In any case, he liked the sound of his own voice and was quite pleased to 'Blow the Man Down'.

Lady Victoria in her high falsetto suddenly launched into 'Silver Threads among the Gold', and the Major's wife joined in, in a brisk no-nonsense voice; but the great thing was, they all *sang*. Even Aileen got up out of her chair to stand by the piano and contributed a low sweet warble. There was no longer any need to 'entertain' them.

Between songs they chattered like school-children. As they thumbed over the song books they reminded each other of old favourites. 'Oh, d'you remember this one? How does it go? *Tum-tum-tum!* "The Dear Little Shamrock".' Miss Calder became as animated as the rest at 'Gaudeamus Igitur' and they were all in full flood, belting out, 'There's One More River to Cross', when I was aware of a sinister sound.

'Pssst!'

It was Oor Net, her cap awry, peering round the door. 'Pssst! What aboot the boofy?' she asked in a loud whisper.

I had forgotten all about the food, and the guests seemed in no hurry to eat. In the end I had to hound them downstairs to partake of the feast; but, even as they ate, they were so wound up they still hummed snatches of the old tunes.

They did not pass any remarks about the food (but that was their style), yet I was pleased to see they ate it as if they enjoyed it. Mother would be sure to ask for details, and I could tell her Lady Victoria had two helpings of boiled ham and the Major licked his lips over the trifle. The Colonel wandered round the table, picking items at random to put on his crowded plate, humming 'The Road to Mandalay' between bites. He ate in a topsy-turvy fashion: apple-tart and cheese, then back to ham and tongue. As usual, I ate nothing, but I could fill up the empty corners later with bread-and-butter.

Oor Net whisked plates to and fro, bamboozled by all the talking and singing, abandoning hope for her cap and not knowing when to curtsey. It was all so easy and informal, I could not believe we were actually entertaining the gentry at last. And that the evening was a success.

No doubt about it!

When the doorbell rang to herald the arrival of the Major's chauffeur, they all gave dismayed sighs. 'But we wanted to go upstairs again and have some more music . . .'

Lady Victoria on the doorstep turned to me and said, 'Thank you, my dear. I can't remember when I've spent such a pleasant evening.' And she meant it.

H.J. sat down at the dining-room table to polish off the trifle and sighed with satisfaction. 'Well, that was a good night! I'm glad I thought of it.'

Oh well! Never mind who took the credit. The great thing was that it was OVER and everyone was pleased.

3. Drama!

By now I was finding out that the parishioners were
real people, not just vague names and faces, and that
Jessie was right when she declared there was nothing
as queer as folk.

For example, Mrs Sturrock, the chief elder's wife,
and Mrs Simpson, the treasurer of the Woman's
Guild, were bosom friends. They were both well-
endowed in that direction. But what puzzled me was
why they miscalled each other behind their backs. It
seemed a strange way of being friendly.

Any time I went down the street there they were
with their heads together talk-talk-talking; and they
were forever ringing each other up, though they
lived only two doors apart, if an item of gossip came
their way. 'Listen to this! Have you heard the latest?'

It seemed on the surface they were in perfect harmony. Yet, if I met them separately, either one or the other would have something spiteful to say about her friend. Indeed, I once asked Mrs Sturrock: 'Do you not like Mrs Simpson?'

Mrs Sturrock looked at me in surprise. 'Oh yes, I like her. We're great friends. But she's an awful liar. D'you know what she told me yesterday . . .?'

I tried to be impartial and not become embroiled in their petty squabbles. Never take sides, I warned myself. Keep your own doorstep clean. Else they would be on the telephone to each other. 'D'you know what she said? Her up at the Manse! Wait till I tell you . . .'

Though I learned to bite my tongue, I sometimes wished H.J. would preach a sermon on the subject. Surely there were plenty of suitable texts in the Good Book. In the Blesseds, for example; or one of Jessie's maxims: 'Haud your wheeshts!'

I imagined having a shot at a sermon myself, thundering from the pulpit and banging the dust out of the big Bible while threatening to send sinners to hell; but the nearest I got to preaching was when I had to take the chair at a Guild meeting. At first I was petrified at the prospect of opening and closing the meeting with prayer. I was given a small devotional book from which I was expected to read out appropriate extracts. They were stilted and meaningless and, as time went by, I grew bold enough to make up my own prayers.

Whether God listened or not, my audience sat up and took notice. From the corner of my eye I could see them nudging each other, and afterwards there was a great deal of whispered speculation. 'Where did she get *that*? Is it the Old Testament or the New?'

It was my own testament. Surely, religion wasn't just in the Bible; it was here in the parish. So I said a few words about everyday things, even mentioning local names. My objective was to be less remote, more homely. It wasn't much, but at least they listened; and now and then I got in a dig of my own. I hoped the Lord would forgive me!

One day I aimed my shaft directly at the two 'friends', not mentioning them by name but begging the Almighty to bless those who guarded their tongues and did not give way to slander. I got so carried away I lapsed into Jessie's tongue and ended by saying it was better to haud oor wheeshts. Amen!

My listeners were dumbfounded at my praying in braid Scots. Mrs Sturrock came bustling up to me and whispered: 'My! You fairly hit the right spot! I hope Mrs Simpson took it all in. I could tell you were thinking of *her!* D'you know what she had the nerve to tell me yesterday . . ?'

So my words fell on stony ground.

Came the day when the two false friends arrived on the Manse doorstep together. This is it, I thought! I would be forced to act as referee for one of their silly squabbles. Help me! I implored the Almighty.

But to my relief they were in perfect harmony and both talking together. Mrs Sturrock spoke louder. 'You remember I rang you up about the Dramatics?'

'No,' I said flatly.

'And you said Yes,' shouted Mrs Simpson, getting her oar in.

'No!' I repeated.

'But you did!' insisted Mrs Sturrock.

'I've got your name down in the book.' Mrs Simpson flourished a tattered jotter at me.

'You'd better come in,' I sighed; at this point they both tried to force their way through the door.

'We're stuck,' gasped Mrs Simpson, heaving against her friend.

'So I see!'

'Tuts! Not now,' said Mrs Sturrock, using her elbows.

'For the Dramatics,' explained Mrs Simpson, pushing past her.

H.J. was fiddling away in the study so I took them into the morning-room, the nearest refuge. There, they gave me chapter and verse, the one interrupting the other. What they were stuck for, it transpired, was a policeman. Would I take the part?

'A bobby? Oh no! I couldn't.'

'Oh yes, you could!' They both spoke with one united voice.

'There's nothing to it,' enlarged Mrs Sturrock. 'You could borrow Baxter's uniform.'

'OH NO! I couldn't.' Baxter was the local policeman who had little to do but stand at the crossroads flexing his muscles. 'He's miles bigger than I am.'

'But we can easily adjust the uniform,' they insisted.

'Then why can't *you* take the part?' I asked, looking from one to the other.

They exchanged glances and confessed, '*We* couldn't get into the uniform. You'll have to do it! It's all arranged.'

'OH NO!'

I tried to fight back, but no amount of 'Oh no's' would wear them down. They were both so big and overpowering that my flame flickered and dwindled out. I didn't actually say Yes, only that I would think about it.

It was enough! 'That's settled then,' said Mrs Simpson, triumphantly jotting it down in her notebook.

'We'll get in touch with you about the rehearsals,' promised Mrs Sturrock; and away they went, colliding in the door on the way out.

I brooded about it for a while, appalled at the prospect of appearing on the stage in such a guise; then I determined to put it at the back of my mind. Why spoil my young life thinking of my deathbed? Though I would sooner be an angel than a policeman. So, apart from the odd glance at P.C. Baxter as he stood at the crossroads, ('OH NO! I couldn't') I succeeded in erasing it from my mind. There were much more pressing problems to face: the minister's frayed cuffs; how to keep Baa-Baa from climbing the stairs to the drawing-room; what to give the Brethren when they came to tea. Oh! hundreds of puzzles.

I had completely forgotten about it when Mrs Sturrock rang up one evening in a state of urgency. I was flummoxed when she asked, 'Can I borrow the minister's trousers?'

'He's out, and he's wearing them himself,' I told her. 'What do you want them for?'

'The rehearsal tonight. You'd better hurry; we're waiting for you. We've got Baxter's uniform for you and a wee moustache . . .'

'OH NO!'

Mrs Sturrock went on relentlessly. 'You can surely find another pair of the minister's trousers.

He's the right size for Maggie Allan who's a post-man . . .'

The only pair I could find in a hurry were his 'whites', the trousers he wore when playing tennis. H.J. was not too pleased to get them back covered with spilt tea and a dab of grease-paint. 'I'll wash them,' I promised. 'Maybe the paint'll come off.' But I doubted it.

I looked terrible in the bobby's uniform fastened together with safety-pins, and with a small moustache wobbling on my upper lip. Thankfully, I had little to say apart from, 'I arrest you in the name of the law,' when I hauled off Maggie Allan clutching H.J.'s trousers. I hit her too hard over the head with Baxter's baton and she let out some words that were not in the script. But this was only a rehearsal. We would be perfect on the night, Mrs Sturrock assured us. I knew she was lying.

By that time she and Mrs Simpson were not on speaking terms. I have forgotten the reason why, but it made life difficult for the rest of us who had to act as go-betweens. 'Tell Mrs Sturrock the curtain's stuck!' Mrs Simpson hissed. 'I warned her it would.' The curtains were Mrs Sturrock's drawing-room ones and I could see Mrs Simpson was quite pleased with this calamity, though it had to be rectified at once. 'Tell Mrs Simpson they need a good tug!' was Mrs Sturrock's reply. 'Wait! I'll come and do it myself.'

It went on like this while the rest of us scuttled about back-stage with problems of our own. Mine were the minister's shoes. I had left the Manse in such a rush there had been no time to ask if I could borrow them; and he clearly had not been able to find another pair for, when I appeared on stage, I saw him sitting in the front row wearing his sandshoes. He never looked at me, only glowered at my feet. It nearly made me forget my cue.

We were dreadful in the play, though I was cheered to the echo every time I appeared on stage. What the previous Lady of the Manse would have thought of my antics I dared not contemplate. I'm in it, I thought, so I might as well act the part. But how to look like Baxter? He sat in his mufti gazing open-mouthed at me and clapped louder than anybody when I hitched up his trousers and twirled his baton. In a way, I suppose, he felt *he* was doing the acting.

Flushed with success, the two friends – Mrs Sturrock and Mrs Simpson – buried the hatchet and clasped hands at the last curtain call. Then they talked mouthfuls of excited words to each other and went home with linked arms.

But that was not the end of it. Oh no!

The acting bug bit the two friends so deeply that they accepted every invitation to perform in neighbouring villages; for, of course, our fame had spread. They even had the effrontery to enter for the Cup. This was a trophy competed for by all drama teams in the county, with an adjudicator to assess the performances and a silver cup to be awarded to the winners.

All that winter I had two identities. At night I was forced to trail round village halls arresting Maggie Allan in the name of the law, while through the day I pursued my more ladylike duties at the Manse. The minister grumbled about having to wear his sand-shoes so often, and P.C. Baxter was constantly in and out of his uniform. I forgot to give it back on one occasion and put him in an awkward situation when his superior officer paid an unexpected visit and caught him in his dungarees. But it was all in the cause of Drama.

I never did get the hang of my moustache which either fell off during the performance or remained so firmly fixed that one night I went to bed wearing it. I had forgotten all about it till Oor Net took one hor-rified look at me in the morning and gasped, 'Holy Moses! have ye saw your face?'

It took a great deal of steeping in boiling water be-fore I could get it off, after which I gave up wearing it and just pencilled one on. By that time I wasn't caring what I looked like; I just went on stage and acted as well as I could.

The morning after our final performance I was surprised to hear H.J. ask, 'How did you get on last night?'

'Last night?' I said vaguely. I was concentrating on pouring out his tea and was so thankful it was all over that I had already put it to the back of my mind.

'The Cup!' H.J. reminded me impatiently.

'Oh that!' I said, passing him *his* cup. 'We won it.'

'What?' H.J. spilt his tea and almost fell off his chair. 'You didn't! Where is it?' He would not believe me till he saw it with his own eyes.

'On the dining-room sideboard. At least, that's where I left it last night.' He had to rush away to make sure. 'It's just a Cup,' I told him. 'It doesn't belong to me. Anyway, you'll get your shoes back now.'

Best of all, it was over. 'But wait till next time,' Mrs Sturrock had said last night in the euphoria of winning. No, no! Never again! No amount of cajoling would induce me to tread the boards once more!

'Wait and see!' said Mrs Simpson darkly.

She and Mrs Sturrock continued their on-off friendship, catter-battering one moment and being lovey-dovey the next. I gave up trying to figure it out. Perhaps it was like the Dramatics and they were both playing parts.

But oh! it was great to see P.C. Baxter back on duty wearing his own uniform, even though it did look as if it had been through the Battle of Bannockburn. I felt the Cup should, by rights, belong to him.

Then one day Oor Net knocked the stuffing out of me by rushing in with hot news.

'Jings Geordie! Ye'll never guess! D'ye ken what Baxter's went an' did? He's grown a moustache!'

Well, imitation is the sincerest form . . .

4. Sick-Visiting

When I first came to the parish I was dumbfounded to discover that the chief topic of conversation was illness.

I did not go in much for illness myself. Jessie had taught me how to put up with pain, ignore sore tummies and be stoical about collywobbles. 'Dinna think aboot them an' they'll gang awa',' was her advice. Ten to one they did, through sheer neglect.

But the parishioners nurtured their ailments and talked endlessly about them, however trivial: boils, bunions, warts, carbuncles, fallen arches, even constipation. Fancy mentioning that! Jessie would have been appalled.

I found it difficult to compete, having only the vaguest notion of the different parts of the human anatomy. Tappits? No! That was part of a motor-car! Kidneys? Were they back or front? Distemper? Was that just dogs? And where on earth was a gall-bladder?

I tried to visualize a tattered book we kept in the kitchen drawer at home: *Till the Doctor Comes*. The advice it gave was generally, 'Keep the patient quiet,' which Jessie interpreted as, 'Haud your wheesht!' Usually it fell open at the measles, but surely it must contain more exciting diseases. Leprosy? The palsy? Or were they just in the Bible? Big ends? No! That was back to the motor-car.

I gave up when asked about my health and just said, 'Me? I'm fine!' though sometimes I longed to boast about the bubonic plague. Better still, an operation. That would have put me on a pedestal.

When Miss Steele, the organist, achieved it, her stock rose sky-high. She was so popular when she had her internals removed that she ousted Mrs Sturrock's ingrowing toenails and Mrs Scott's varicose veins. When she came home from hospital Miss Steele kept her X-ray pictures on the mantelpiece, and the neighbours called in to gaze at them as if they were Old Masters. Proud woman, she had scars to show to favoured visitors. How could one compete with that?

The District Nurse was perpetually pedalling from door to door on her bicycle, dealing with minor ailments. Though Miss Paterson was a no-nonsense woman, she knew that listening patiently was as effective as a soothing ointment.

'Oh yes! You've had a terrible time, poor soul; but

41

you're on the mend. Keep sucking the lozenges and I'll be in to see you tomorrow.'

Only in severe cases did she advise getting the doctor. As Dr Trollope did not live in the district this involved a great deal of palaver before an appointment could be made; but how proud the patients were to spread the tidings! 'Oh yes! It's serious. I'm getting the doctor.'

In spite of his literary name, Dr Trollope was a man of few words, with little time for malingerers. His small talk was short and sharp. 'Cough! Put out your tongue! Say ninety-nine! That's all right! You'll live!'

If he prescribed medicine, his patient kept the bottle of coloured liquid on the window-sill for all passers-by to see. 'Yes! She's still under the doctor. Three times daily after meals.' Personally, the thought of getting Dr Trollope would be enough to cure me of the most dread disease.

The parishioners always asked me, 'How's the minister?' and I always said, 'Fine!' for if I varied it by saying, 'He's got a wee cough,' that would bring forth a deluge of suggested remedies: hot poultices, cold compresses, toddy, a stocking tied round the throat, a boiled onion, gargle with salty water, put him to bed.

If H.J. had a genuine sore throat I just dosed him with the family palliative which was unfailing – a hot blackcurrant drink – and took the odd sip myself because I liked the taste.

There was really no time to be off-colour in the Manse or to wonder if we were feeling well or ill. It was only when someone else noticed it, that we began to feel a bit 'queer'. When Wee Wullie passed

on his German measles to me, I was vaguely aware
of having a struggle to keep going, but I kept sol-
diering on till Mrs Sturrock, meeting me in the
street, said, 'My! You look terrible! I think you're
sickening!' At which point I began to feel woozy.

I went home and filled a hot-water-bottle. As I
was climbing the stairs with it under my arm, I
bumped into Oor Net coming down. 'Holy Moses!'
she gasped. 'Where are ye gaun?'

'To my bed for a wee while,' I said dizzily. 'You
can make the minister's supper.'

'Jehovah!' cried Nettie, following me into the
bedroom. 'What'll I make?'

'Oh! just something . . . toasted eggs.'

'What's toasted eggs?' Oor Net wanted to know.

I shook my head for I did not know myself, and
lay down on top of the bed.

'Oh Lord!' Oor Net regarded me with horror,
then rose to the occasion. 'Keep the heid! I'll do
something. Dinna budge!'

I lay still but the bed budged. It seemed suddenly
overcome by a fit of the shivers, shaking and shoog-
ling as if possessed. Meanwhile, I was aware of loud
household noises from down below: the front doorbell ringing, the back door banging, Bush barking,
and Oor Net pitching her voice. When I opened my
eyes she was looming over me.

'It's thon man aboot the linoleum,' she hissed
under her breath, not to disturb me. 'An' Wee
Wullie's fell aff the dyke an' hurted his knee. The
sink's clogged, an' the meenister'll just have to eat
scones for his supper. Canny find ony eggs. Dinna
budge!'

A few minutes later I found myself on my feet. I

went and sat on the stairs for a while. Bush came and licked my hand, and presently Nettie brought me a cup of tea. Then suddenly I pulled myself together and felt better. So maybe Jessie was right. 'Dinna think aboot it, an' it'll gang awa'.'

But oh! there were times when I was heartily sick of sick-visiting. It was one of the musts of Manse-folk, never to be neglected. H.J. often passed it on to me as a suitable task for a 'lady'. 'You'd better go and see Mrs Brown. She's got a bad cough.' Or, 'Tell Miss Macfarlane I'll call in when I can. She wasn't at church on Sunday and the elder thinks she should be visited.'

So I had to set off on my mission of mercy, often crossing endless fields to reach a faraway cottage. Sometimes I would surprise the invalid out chopping sticks or hanging up the washing. When she saw me she would start coughing and pulling her shawl round her shoulders. 'I've been awful poorly,' she would wheeze. 'The District Nurse comes every day. If it doesn't clear up, I'll have to get the doctor.'

I tried to put on a sympathetic expression and to refuse a cup of tea. But, 'Och! there's no hurry,' she would say, drawing me into the house. (No hurry for her!) Then I would be forced to sit and listen to every single symptom from the moment she woke up one morning with a 'sair thrapple', which was her version of a sore throat.

I tried to divert the conversation into other channels by recounting any happening that came into my head and was sometimes rewarded with, 'My! you've fairly cheered me up.' But the invalid always reverted to her cough on parting. 'Be sure to tell the minister I've been awful bad.' 'Oh yes, I will! He'll be very worried.'

I recalled Jessie's old saying (when was I not remembering Jessie?), 'Never visit onybody withoot a crookit oxter,' which meant always carry a gift under your arm; so I tried to take a 'minding' with me. Often I just picked some wild flowers on the way and stuck them in an empty jam-jar to cheer the patient. Or I put some home-made parkins in a paper poke, if my baking had turned out to be edible.

What they all wanted, I realized, was to be noticed. 'Look at *me!* I'm somebody special.' But I was only a substitute and they would have been better pleased with the minister. So I had to lay it on thick. 'He's a bit busy today, but he sent a message to say he hoped you'd soon be better. I was to be sure to tell you he missed seeing you in church last Sunday.'

That perked up the invalid who promised, 'Yes, I'll be there! Tell the minister.' Then she would say to her neighbours, '*She* came with a message from the minister.' Recognition had been achieved!

Just now and again I had a small reward when one of them greeted me with, 'Och! I'm glad it's you, lassie.' Then she would whisper behind her hand, 'There's some things I canna tell the meenister.'

So I had my uses.

And how grateful I was at the end of the day to be agile enough to run up the Manse stairs two at a time to reach the sanctuary of my bedroom. Now at last I could be myself behind the shut door, not the Lady of the Manse. It was bliss to scribble in my jotter or read till the book dropped from my hand.

But even here there was no certainty of being safe from interruptions. Sometimes the jangle of the doorbell woke me in the wee sma' hoors, and I knew it to be an urgent summons from someone dying or in distress. Automatically, I scrambled out of bed, put on my shabby dressing-gown and slid down the banisters in the darkness, while Bush came sleepily out of the kitchen and accompanied me to the front door. An elder would be there with a torch in his hand.

'Is the minister in?'

'Yes, of course!' Where else would he be at this hour?

'It's Mrs Bell. She's far through.'

'Right! I'll get him'.

Give him his due, H.J. shook off his slumbers without a grumble and was up and out in a twinkling. I hung about and kept the kettle on the boil till he came back. One look at his face and I knew. Sometimes he just shook his head, so I put extra sugar in his tea and knew there would be a funeral in the offing.

The walled-in graveyard was some distance from the kirk, with mossy stones lying toppled on the grass, their angels' wings broken, and with faded inscriptions too difficult to read. The entire family was there, with Father at the top, and 'Jessica, beloved wife of the above' underneath. Then came the children, some sadly 'died in infancy'. I tried to decipher the verses, hoping I might find a comical one:

> Here lies interred a man o' micht.
> His name was Michael Downie.
> He lost his life one merket nicht
> By tummlin' aff his pownie.

I could only make out scraps: 'Gone to heaven.' 'Rest in peace.' 'Sadly missed.' And one extolled the virtues of the deceased: 'An upright man till God felled him.' I pictured the Almighty wielding a great hammer and shouting, 'Take that, Geordie Burns!'

Some newer stones stood upright with fresh flowers at their base, and sometimes I saw a black-clad figure steal in to lay a bunch on a grave, lingering with bowed head to say a private prayer. Leckie was the gravedigger and it was one of his tasks to keep the grounds tidy and 'fit for the deid'.

But a graveyard was not considered a fit place for women. They could attend the service held in a bereaved household, but they had to stay behind while the men followed the hearse to the graveside.

Occasionally it was my duty to attend a funeral service in some remote cottage, crowding into the parlour along with the rest while the minister prayed over the coffin. The widow-woman sat silent, looking down at her hands, while the men shuffled their feet uneasily and avoided each other's eyes. Then came the solemn carrying out of the coffin on its last journey.

Left behind, what could one say to the bereft widow? Sometimes I just sat and held her hand, or tried to distract her by suggesting something practical to keep her occupied. 'What about getting out some more cups?' Or, 'D'you think you've cut enough bread?' Having something to do helped to get her over the first hurdle.

But if she wanted to talk, I was there to listen. One old woman brought out the family album and took me through every stage of her life, while her husband was being buried.

'Look! That's him in his kilt. At the war.'

'Oh! He was nice-looking,' I remarked. As, indeed, he was: a sturdy upstanding youth.

Then came the wedding-group, all stiff and unsmiling. What could I say? 'I like your hat. What colour was it?'

'Blue,' she said, brightening up, 'with a wee feather at the side.' The old eyes began to shine as she recalled the great day. 'We went to M'Auntie Jean's in Berwick for the honeymoon . . .' And she was off, re-living that long-ago occasion. If a few tears fell they were happier ones and quickly brushed away. Sometimes I dropped a tear myself out of genuine sympathy; then I would say briskly, 'Is that kettle not boiling? The men'll be back soon.'

When the men returned they shook hands with the widow and mumbled something. If there was a male relative to take charge, he would produce some glasses and a bottle while the women passed round the ham sandwiches. Gradually tongues were loosened and an occasional guffaw of laughter was heard; then, remembering the solemnity of the occasion, it was quickly stifled. Between drams, the men would sigh and remark to each other, 'A'weel, that's Bob awa'. A decent chap.' Whose turn would it be next? Better refill their glasses and banish such thoughts. So the melancholy occasion often ended in forced gaiety.

The women stayed behind to help with the clearing up. It was the only time the widow-woman had not washed her own dishes and she looked ill-at-ease, sitting with idle hands. 'No, no!' she would protest. 'That teapot gangs on the top shelf. Watch oot! Ye'll drop it!'

I tried to make follow-up visits, knowing the worst time was after all the excitement had died down and the bereaved woman was left staring at an empty armchair and a neglected pipe on the mantelpiece. It was best to talk of ordinary things. Were the hens laying? And had she heard the school windows were broken? Would she like me to fetch in some logs for the fire?

The minister, too, made special visits and brought her a different kind of comfort, I hoped. I wondered if he 'put up a prayer'. Perhaps he did not talk about religion at all. Whatever his methods he always succeeded and before long the widow would be back in her pew on Sundays. It was all part of his job as 'the minister'.

But och! I could not always dwell on such morbid matters. What would life be without a funny-bone? There was a comical side even to chronic ailments.

Old Sarah Googly, crippled with 'arthuritis', never gave in to it.

'It'll no' get the better o' me,' she declared defiantly; though now and again she made a wry face and muttered, 'Bodies are a pest! Isn't it a peety we canna be born withoot them?'

5. Manse Mice

There's nothing so poor as a church mouse – a *kirk moose* Leckie called it – but the 'mice' who lived in Manses were often as hard put to make ends meet.

I used to imagine that all Manse children must be wee angels. How could they help being good, living in such a holy atmosphere? On the contrary, I soon found out that most of them were wee deevils. It was the reaction, I suppose.

I had some sympathy with them, having been a wee deevil myself. What young thing could keep up a façade of perfection for ever? In public they were forced to be pillars of propriety; never fidget in the Manse pew, never make funny faces, never stick out their tongues, never be natural. All eyes were upon them and they must set an example to ordinary children.

Inwardly they were seething with suppressed wickedness which often found an outlet in underhand ploys. Below the pew they stuck pins in each other or tried to fire pellets from hidden catapults. And the moment they were set free, they let off steam by kicking and scratching like wild animals, always taking care to put on an innocent face if found out. Poor things! They were forced to lead double lives, the good and the bad; and, of course, it was the bad they liked best.

When I visited other Manses in the neighbourhood the children recognized a fellow-sufferer and took me into their confidence. They showed me the contents of their pooches, much the same as those of any lively child – white mice, pocket-knives, toy pistols, string, nails, safety-pins – and boasted about their wicked exploits. When I asked one of these unruly lads if he was going to follow in his father's footsteps when he grew up, he gave me a withering look and scoffed, 'Don't be daft! I'd sooner be a burglar!'

But time no doubt would tame them, and the notion of becoming tinkers or tramps wear off. Likely, some of them became eminent preachers in due course; but oh! I did sympathize with them when they were young and caged.

Not so much, though, as I pitied their mothers. How often *they* must have felt like running away! But where could they run? They were trapped for life.

The first thing I noticed when we called at neighbouring Manses was that every minister's wife had red work-roughened hands; and that the strain of keeping up an appearance of shabby gentility was ageing them before their time.

I used to think my own lot hard till I met Mrs

Purves, the first Manse lady I got to know inti-
mately. She and her husband lived in the next parish
and, as well as meeting on official occasions, we
gradually became acquainted with them as human
beings.

When we were first invited to tea I recognized all
the signs of stress on Mrs Purves's face: the family-
hold-back attitude at the tea-table, the apologies for
the untidy room, and the look of resignation when
she had to get up to answer the doorbell. Her husband, I could see, was nice but handless. It never occurred to him to rush to the kitchen for more hot
water, or to mop up the milk when one of the children upset the jug. He was God's man, living on a
higher plane, and could shut himself in the study
while the dirdum of the house raged over his head. It
was up to the Lady to sort out mundane matters.
That was why he had married her. As well as for
love, I hoped.

When the two reverends went out for a stroll in
the overgrown garden I offered to wash the dishes.
'Oh no! The kitchen's in a terrible mess,' she
protested.

'That'll make me feel at home,' I said, rolling up
my sleeves.

Her servant-lassie was off with exhaustion, she
told me, looking exhausted herself, and the hot-
water system wasn't working; but we managed
with kettles and, after we had cleared up, went back
to the cluttered sitting-room.

It was then Mrs Purves let down her hair, though
her hands were automatically busy with the contents
of her darning-basket. She had five children and
another on the way. 'One more mouth to feed,' she

said with a shrug of her shoulders. But thank goodness she had a funny-bone, and there were tears of
laughter in her eyes as she recounted some of the
comical episodes in the life of a minister's wife.

I warmed to her as we laughed together and,
whenever I felt at the end of my tether, I thought of
Mrs Purves and my own burdens seemed lighter.

On the practical side, she was the first 'lady' to
give me tips on how to run a Manse economically,
how to save light and heat, how to stretch a meagre
ration of meat – I use some of her recipes to this day
– how to concoct nourishing puddings, to mend and
patch, and best of all how to handle difficult
parishioners. 'I just smile at them and say nothing,'
Mrs Purves told me. 'Luckily they can't hear what
I'm thinking!'

In return I lent her books and, more importantly,
a listening lug. As we chatted I helped her with the
mending, for she was constantly refurbishing gar-
ments for her growing family; and sometimes I took
over the task of putting her brood to bed.

I could cuff the wee deevils, tell them stories, and
do a Jessie on them; so we got on fine. 'Are you a
lady?' one of them asked while I was hauling him out
from under the bed.

'No, I'm not! I'm just a lassie!' I said. 'Come out
and I'll tell you a story.'

It was a sure way of keeping them quiet. Five pairs
of eyes would be focused on me as the children hung
on every word. The trouble was getting away; for
no sooner had a story ended than they would try to
prolong the agony of going to sleep by pleading,
'Go on! Begin again at the beginning.'

I had to assume a stern expression as I tucked them

in. 'No more just now. I'll tell you another next
time.'

'When?'

'Oh! . . . soon!' And they were asleep as soon as I
had tiptoed away.

Apart from Mrs Purves, I found most Manse
ladies much of a muchness, all down-to-earth
women wearing sensible clothes and trying to hide
the darns in their gloves. Their resigned looks
touched my heart, and I wondered what they might
have been if they could have followed their own inclinations instead of being subservient to their husbands. But perhaps they were content with their lot.
And in those days none of us had heard of women's
lib.

True, some seemed proud to be first ladies in their
parish. It gave them a standing in the community
but, with such a high price to pay, they soon lost
their airs and graces in their efforts to keep up ap-
pearances while working harder than any common

parishioner. And soon they gave up the struggle and became 'ordinary' themselves.

They had always to remember His Reverence was the important one. Yet, without such hard-working helpmates, ministers would have found it difficult to survive. We were all necessary – you in your small corner and I in mine – so I tried to do my share, though determined to cling to my own identity. Mrs Purves was right: no one could stop us from thinking.

The difficulty was finding time to think of anything but immediate problems. I had to keep a firm hold on myself to avoid daydreaming as I walked up the street, otherwise I risked bumping into parishioners. In a daydream, I had a bottomless purse and could concoct splendid meals for the Purves family, with second or even third helpings for all. ('Oh sorry, Mrs Simpson! Are you keeping well?')

The only exception to the run-of-the-mill ladies lived near Berwick, and we sometimes called in to see her on our expeditions to the big city. Mrs Kennedy did not obey any of the unwritten rules. She had no aptitude for Manse life and made no pretence about it. She did not even try to look the part, but wore dainty shoes with high heels, dashing hats which she fashioned herself, and a cloak!

As for humdrum parish duties, she ignored them in favour of her own pursuits: flower-arranging, poetry, embroidery and water-colours. She could never be bothered to bake or dust, far less teach in the Sunday-school, so she was the 'speak' of the district. The other Manse ladies frowned on her, though secretly envying her independence, and I thought she was wonderful. Why not have a decorative lady for a change?

I did wonder how her husband had caught such a *rara avis*. He had a crumpled air about him – no wonder, since he had to iron his own shirts – but he plainly adored his wife and never tried to restrain her excesses, beyond a mild protest, 'Now, Rita!' But Rita just smiled at him and went her own way.

I was never on Rita terms with her and never got to know her well, though I would have welcomed an opportunity to talk to her, or rather listen. But I sometimes acted Martha to her Mary when she had forgotten to bring things from the kitchen.

'Oh dear! is that just water in the pot? No tea!' Or, 'If you look in the oven, you *might* find a tart there. Did I put it in, I wonder?' But whatever else she forgot, she always remembered to put a posy of flowers on the table, a feast for the eyes. Even ministers did not live by bread alone.

Perhaps it was just as well Mrs Kennedy was out of my orbit or I might have been carried away by her airy-fairy notions. Instead, I tried to learn from the sensible Manse ladies whose talk was all about pinching and paring. The things they did for economy's sake! Turn collars and cuffs, eke out soap, patch slippers, even mend bootlaces, save paper, save everything!

I did not have to go to such extremes myself since I had no squad of hungry children to feed and clothe, and was lucky in getting occasional gifts from the farm when Father and Mother visited us: butter and cheese, spare-ribs if the pig had been killed, and sometimes a side of bacon. It was a hunger or a burst; and, though I was not a good manager, I tried to be prepared for droppers-in by keeping 'something in the tins' for tea when unexpected visitors called.

The Manse ladies, I found, were not borrowers; they were all in the same boat. So it was a pleasure for me to share my farm fare with Mrs Purves or one of the other ladies when I received a windfall. And our own parishioners, especially the gentry, sometimes left surprise treats on the doorstep – a pheasant or a salmon – to add sparkle to the menu. But on the whole we existed on plain fare and did without what we could not get. It was good for the soul.

'And Mrs Kennedy gives her cat *cream!*' sighed Mrs Purves, but without envy, making the most of skim milk.

Miss Calder from next door, reputed to be 'rolling in money' though I saw no evidence of it, was different in that she not only borrowed but was annoyed if I did not instantly produce what she wanted. 'I'm sorry, Miss Calder. I haven't any ground almonds.' 'No ground almonds! Tuts!' – and I would be made to feel incompetent, as indeed I was.

On Sundays we 'ladies' all sat in the Manse pews with pious looks on our faces and practical thoughts in our minds. 'Give us this day our daily bread . . . and what the dickens can we put on it? Mercy! It's high time I was making marmalade . . .'

Sometimes I glanced at the minister. What were his thoughts as he sat back burying his face in his hands, waiting for the collection to be taken? 'I might manage a game of golf tomorrow . . . thank goodness we've been invited out to supper tonight. That means a good spread . . . Blessings on thy gifts,

O Lord!'

We were only human.

I did try to remember God was in the kirk count-
ing every hair on my head, so presumably He was
aware of the state of the Manse larder. It was best to
think of other folk and ignore one's own problems.
Help Mrs Moffat out of her pew. 'How are the
rheumatics today? Oh yes! I'll tell the minister you
enjoyed his sermon . . .'

We were lucky having four wheels. Most ministers had only two, and wobbled about on creaky
bicycles when visiting their flock. Often they were
to be seen at the roadside mending a tyre, or pedalling wearily home in the darkness with their
acetylene lights flickering. A sturdy pair of legs was
as essential to a minister as a good grounding in
Hebrew.

I knew nothing of Hebrew but was thankful my
legs were strong enough, for though I sometimes
travelled in my brother's Baby Austin it broke down
oftener than not and I had to take to my feet while he
was tinkering with its innards. Sometimes I
squeezed through a hedge and took a short-cut across the fields, arriving back at the Manse before the
'baby' came spluttering home. Indeed, I often refused his offer of a lift. 'No, thanks! I'll just walk.' It
was quicker and saved all the bother of helping to
haul the car out of a rut.

'Where's the minister?' I was often asked as I
wended my way home alone.

'In the ditch,' was my invariable reply.

But eventually he would arrive back and his first
query was, 'What's for supper?'

I wished I could ask him the same question when I

returned from a weary spell of sick-visiting. 'Don't be long!' he would say hungrily. 'I'm starving!'

I had been mentally making the supper all the way home. Sausages and fried potatoes? Eggs, poached, scrambled, or what? Cheese-pudding? A tin of something . . .? He might at least have had the kettle boiling!

Then I thought of the other Manse ladies with their much bigger problems and realized how lucky I was. I might even surprise H.J. by picking a spray of candytuft to cheer up the supper-table.

6. Verily, Verily

When the doorbell rang that morning I swallowed one of Oor Net's expletives, but she let go.

'Holy Moses! An' us in the middle o' the sheets!' (Washing them, she meant.)

As this was washing-day I had no intention of answering the summons. Let H.J. go. He was mooning in the study, practising golf-shots prior to joining some cronies for their Monday round. It was a good way of getting rid of religion after his busy Sunday. I had to get rid of mine by tackling the sheets.

Wash-day was potluck day at the Manse when I did little cooking beyond heating up yesterday's soup and putting a pot of stovies at the side of the range. Nettie and I had enough to do, pumping up water for the boiler, rubbing and scrubbing the clothes, then putting them through the mangle to get rid of the bulk of the water. There were no mod. cons. in the Manse and we were both up to the elbows in soapy suds. Indeed, Nettie was so wet I could have wrung her out with the sheets, and the kitchen was in such a mess even Bush and Baa-Baa had scuttled out of the back door, leaving us to our travails.

'There it's again!' cried Oor Net, as the doorbell gave another jangle. 'Will I answer it?'

'No! Leave it to the minister,' I said, squeezing the suds out of his pyjamas.

Graith Jessie called the suds. I thought back to wash-day at home where we had our own 'steamie' in one of the outhouses and could make as much mess as we liked. It had been fun in those days to help, or rather hinder, the washerwoman as she 'possed' the clothes, pounding them with a wooden battering-ram and sometimes tramping the blankets in her bare feet. But there were no doorbells there to disturb us, only the pig grunting or the turkey-cock pecking at our heels.

The minister waited for the third ring before I heard him trailing along the passage to answer it. Thereafter there was a deadly silence.

'It's naebody!' said Oor Net, busy at the pump.

But why had 'naebody' rung the doorbell? I found out when H.J. appeared in the kitchen with a telegram in his hand and a strange expression on his face.

I felt myself going white. Mercy! I thought, somebody's dead.

'Is it bad news?' I managed to ask.

The telegram in his hand was shaking, and H.J. did not seem to know whether it was bad news or good.

'It's from the Moderator,' said my brother, looking at the trembling telegram. 'He's coming!'

'Jings! When?'

'Today!' said H.J. excitedly. 'He'll likely be expecting lunch.'

'Holy Moses!' I gasped, dripping soapsuds on the floor. I would have sat down if there had been anywhere to sit.

I was used to H.J. bringing unexpected guests for meals; it never occurred to him that meals had to be made. 'How many?' I got into the habit of asking, and managed to stretch the food somehow. Droppers-in were more of a nuisance if H.J. was out and they insisted on waiting to see the minister. Sometimes I felt I could not shut them into the study without trying to 'entertain' them to small talk; but more often I just shoved a book at them – any book – and said, 'Would you like to look at that?' before scuttling back to the kitchen. On one occasion I forgot I had left an elderly gent on his own till Oor Net said, 'There's a funny noise in the study.' When I went in I found him snoring his head off and had to revive him with strong tea before H.J. arrived.

But this was different. The Moderator was the most important man in Scotland; in the world, some ministers thought. To receive a visit from him was tantamount to entertaining royalty. (On yesterday's soup and stovey-tatties!) He was the head man in the kirk, far above ordinary ministers; he presided over the General Assembly in Edinburgh and his term of office involved him in a great deal of pomp and ceremony. His underlings spoke of him with bated breath and every word that fell from his lips was considered a pearl of wisdom.

Small wonder my brother's hands were trembling. It was an accolade for such a new minister to be noticed at all, let alone be favoured with a visit. What should he do first? Change his plus-fours, find his dog-collar, put away his golf clubs, hide the *Sporting Times*, rush up and tidy the drawing-room?

'Have you seen my back-stud?' he wailed, meeting himself coming back. 'And I'll need another pair of socks.'

'Look below the bed,' I said automatically.

I was frozen into inaction, but had to pull myself together. 'Come on!' I said to Oor Net. 'We'll need to do something.'

But Oor Net was too dumbstruck to do anything except gasp, 'Michty God!' Never in her wildest dreams had she imagined seeing someone on a par with the Almighty at close quarters.

Presently she spluttered, 'Will he be wearing his fancies?'

'His fancies?'

Nettie had a mental picture of the Moderator in full fig, as he was at the Assembly, an impressive figure attired in knee-breeches, with ruffles at his neck, frills at his wrists, a ring on his finger, and a look of piety on his face. A Being far and away above the rest of us.

'He'll be wearing something!' I assured her briskly. 'I hope he likes corned beef. It's the only tin left in the cupboard.'

It seemed a poor substitute for oysters and caviare

which would have been more fitting for His Holiness, but it was that or nothing. I watered the soup and pushed the pan of stovies nearer the fire. Then somehow or other I set a meal-for-two on the dining-room table. I could see I would get no help from Oor Net who was still wringing a wet sheet and clutching it to her bosom. I would be forced to serve the meal myself.

There was no time to spruce myself before the doorbell rang. It had scarcely stopped jangling before H.J. was halfway along the passage to answer it, a slipper on one foot and a shoe on the other. I heard voices as the visitor was led into the study, and hoped the door would close so that I could scuttle upstairs and make myself presentable. But presently H.J. came to the kitchen door and announced tersely, 'Better have lunch now! He hasn't got much time.'

'Holy God!' said Oor Net, and stuffed the wet sheet in her mouth.

When I went in to serve the soup H.J. said apologetically, 'This is my sister.' It was plain to see he was ashamed of me.

The Almighty held out his hand and, as I shook it, the first thing I noticed was he was not wearing his fancies. Indeed, he looked like an ordinary man and was as nice as tuppence!

'It's a dreadful day, wash-day,' he said understandingly, seeing my sopping state. 'We men don't know what you have to put up with!' He glanced at H.J. who grinned foolishly. Certainly, *he* didn't know. 'Let me help you with those dishes.'

He was no bother at all.

I could not believe it was the *Moderator* who was

ladling out the soup and passing the plates. All the
while he talked about this and that, and I found myself responding as if he was just anybody. Fancy him
being human! So human he insisted on carrying the
empty plates all the way to the kitchen, a thing H.J.
would never have condescended to do. I could see
Oor Net gasping like a fish out of water as he tried to
find a space amongst the clutter on the kitchen table.

The Moderator did not ignore her, but held out
his hand and said, 'How are *you?*'

'Oh! I'm f-f-fine!' gulped Oor Net, giving him a
soapy handshake and stuffing the wet sheet back in
her mouth.

Before he left with H.J. to have a look at the
church – and my brother was busily putting on his
other shoe – the Moderator patted my unruly locks
and said, 'Thank you. I've got a wee girl of my
own.'

But I wasn't a wee girl; I was a Lady of the Manse.

I sat in the kitchen with Nettie eating corned beef with my fingers and pondering over the simplicity of the Mighty. I could have preached a good sermon there and then, if only I had had the chance.

It had all been too much for Oor Net. The corned beef was sticking to her gullet and she was almost choking with emotion as she recalled the great event. At intervals she kept looking at her hand and muttering, 'Fancy Him shaking it!'

I got fed up with her and said, 'He's only a man.'

'No, he's not!' burst out Nettie. The Moderator only a man!

'He is so!' I insisted. 'He was once a bairn like . . . like Henry John.'

But she would not have it. *He* could never have been a puking child like her wee brother. 'He's mair like . . . Moses!' she declared. 'And he shook ma hand!'

H.J. was almost as bad. Right enough, it was a feather in his cap; and for days afterwards his conversation was punctuated with, 'As I was saying to the Moderator.' His standing rose in the parish and even I had some reflected glory.

I tried to be airy-fairy about it. 'The Moderator? Oh yes, he came to lunch.' I was a little more cagey when asked what he had eaten. The annoying thing was, he had no sooner gone that the Major's chauffeur arrived with a pheasant. But at least we had a good supper.

It came to pass in the fullness of time that Mother rang me up one day and said, 'What about a hat?'

'A hat? I've got one!'

I was always on the defensive with Mother on the

subject of clothes. She would never allow me to choose my own for special occasions, knowing full well I would have opted for scarlet or some unsuitable colour that would not 'go' with my red hair. I was heartily sick of muted shades of greens, blues and browns.

'You'll need a new one,' said Mother firmly.

'What for?'

'Tuts! The General Assembly, of course!' said Mother impatiently. 'You'll have to look respectable when you go to Edinburgh.'

'Oh, help!'

'So we'd better meet in Berwick to choose a new one,' declared Mother.

'You mean *you*'ll choose,' I muttered under my breath.

My current hat was green. It was just a hat and had served me well for Sunday wear. The new one was blue, much the same. It looked 'respectable', but oh! if only it had been red.

H.J. looked spruce enough when we set out. I had dusted him down and polished his shoes – he was wearing both today – determined he should set out looking a credit to his parish. We were accompanied by the chief elder and his wife, Mr and Mrs Sturrock, and travelled by train to avoid any trouble with the temperamental motor-car. This was not a day for heaving the 'baby' out of a ditch or mending burst tyres.

I was suitably subdued as I sat in the compartment wearing my new hat, and with a pair of gloves hiding the blemishes on my work-roughened hands. The Sturrocks had lofty looks on their faces to show they were above the commonality today,

68

and Mrs Sturrock's bosom was so tightly laced I feared there would be an explosion before we reached Edinburgh.

At the Waverley Station I would have liked to throw my hat in the air and run up to see the Floral Clock and all the distractions of the big toon, but I was forced to walk sedately towards the Mound, past John Knox who frowned at me disapprovingly. Had *he* never been young and daft? Not likely!

We left H.J. and the elder to their ministrations, then Mrs Sturrock and I joined the conclave of women thronging to the Guild meeting. Mine was not the only hat, but it was amongst the plainest. The others had toshed up their headpieces as best they could: a feather here, a flower there, a little veil over the eyes. Today they were real Ladies of the Manse. They had never seen a kitchen sink in their lives, and what did it matter that little Bobby's breeks were torn beyond repair? They were not going to mend them today, even mentally.

I recognized a few faces here and there. Mrs Purves, safely delivered of twins, waved to me. She was looking much slimmer. No wonder! How had she disposed of her babes today, and how was she going to feed them? I looked in vain for Mrs Kennedy, but Rita had followed her own inclinations as usual, and was doubtless visiting an Edinburgh art gallery or reading poetry in Princes Street Gardens.

It was no use wishing *I* was free, with Mrs Sturrock sitting bolt upright beside me. I had to help her take notes of the speeches to recount later to our own Guild back home. She had told me it was my bounden duty to listen, so I did my best to concentrate on the earnest ladies on the platform.

Fancy getting up and facing such a throng! My knees were wobbling at the very thought, and I found it difficult to keep my mind on the subjects: the Schemes of the Church, how to help in Foreign Fields, how to support our menfolk. (I wondered if they were discussing how to support *us*.)

The magic moment approached.

This was the highlight of the proceedings – the arrival of the Moderator himself who had come to make a brief speech and give us his blessing. The ladies sat up, adjusted their hats, and held their breath when he appeared. He was wearing his fancies! Oor Net would have swooned at the sight of him: knee-breeches, frills, ruffles and all. Nothing ordinary about him. She had been right! *He* could never have been a bawling bairn like her wee brother, Henry John Hogg. Or eaten corned beef for his lunch.

I bowed my head like the rest, carried away by the solemnity of the occasion. When he left, the ladies whispered to each other appreciatively before settling down to the next item on the agenda. They looked elevated after being in the Presence.

Afterwards I had a cup of tea with Mrs Purves who had left the twins with her sister and was about to rush off to feed them. We spoke of mundane matters but she, too, admitted having been 'taken out of herself'.

'Yes! There's something about these occasions,' she declared, hastily drawing on her gloves as she rose to go. 'I've been to dozens, but there *is* something! I'll have to fly; the twins will be howling.'

I took off my hat in the train going home and tousled my hair. Mrs Sturrock's bosom was de-

flated, but not her tongue. She did not notice that
nobody was listening and her husband was sound
asleep. H.J. was writing indecipherable notes on sermon paper with a 'holy' look on his face till he, too,
fell asleep – and dreamt of golf? He had his customary crumpled look about him when he woke up.

Mrs Sturrock droned on. 'M'm!' I answered now
and again till I became too drowsy myself. Before I
drifted away the inevitable thought flashed through
my mind, 'What's for supper?'

For weeks afterwards Oor Net was sentimental
about the Manse sheets. 'That's the one I was
washin' when *He* came!' she told anyone who would
listen.

And, as if anticipating a Second Coming, I took
care to keep a tin of corned beef in the cupboard.

7. Storms

I made my escapes on the few evenings when I could take to my heels with Bush jumping for joy behind me. I would run along the lane leading to the gentry's houses, hoping to meet Aileen exercising her dog Jasper at a more sedate pace.

It was the only chance we had of jabbering to each other about the craft we had in common. Though Aileen was an 'Honourable' out of the topmost drawer, not a rag-tag-and-bobtail like myself, we were on equal terms when discussing our writing activities. Indeed, sometimes I felt superior for Aileen needed someone to stir her up and spur her on. She was vaguely writing a book about Nell Gwyn (Nelly, we called her) but easily became dispirited, though she had the entire day at her disposal – or perhaps because of it – and I had only odd moments in which to scribble.

'You *must* get on with it,' I urged her. 'It won't write itself. Go home and pick up your pen.' (The pen which the parlourmaid dusted every morning while tidying Aileen's desk.)

As we gabbled, Aileen's gentle voice grew louder till she became almost animated. 'Yes, I will! Yes, I will!' she promised, before I had to tear myself away and speed back to the humdrum duties of the Manse.

Thankfully, Aileen lived long enough to justify my faith in her literary ability. Years later, when we were far apart, I received an ecstatic telegram from her which everyone thought was the announcement of an engagement: NELLY ACCEPTED JOHN LONG. LOVE AILEEN. It was much more than a romance for Aileen who lived to see the book published; and when I look at the frayed copy on my shelves today, I am instantly transported to those stolen moments in that windswept lane.

It was lined with gnarled old trees twined with ivy overcoats and with branches that often bent in the breeze. On one stormy night I was afraid Aileen would also bend, so I accompanied her home and saw her safely indoors before speeding back to the refuge of the Manse.

Sometimes I encountered the eccentric Colonel who still addressed me as 'boy' and whom I always saluted in passing: 'Good evening, sir!' And once I almost bumped into the Pisky Parson, the Episcopalian preacher, accompanied by an elderly woman. His mother, or his wife? She seemed to disapprove of me and called him to heel when he would have lingered for a chat. 'Come along, Albert!' – and he went, as meek as a mouse.

Aileen and I were not the only ones to chatter in that leafy lane. The birds in the branches kept up a constant conversation, and the rooks cawed incessantly as if holding quarrelsome committee meetings. It was here I found the first pale primroses and the last red rowans.

It was my escape-route to freedom.

On the night of the gale we had a missionary staying in the Manse, an inoffensive old gentleman who slept through it all on his deaf ear. I might have done the same on any ear had not the doorbell rung so furiously. I was furious, too, for I had been enjoying one of my 'home' dreams in the byre, listening to Jessie telling a story.

It was the one about Meggy-Mony-Feet, a centipede who got every one of her tootsies stuck in a jar of treacle. Jessie was telling it so vividly I could smell the treacle and see every wrinkle on her face. When the first crash came and Jessie stopped talking, I thought the black-and-white cow had kicked over the milk-pail, but that was not sufficient reason for stopping the story. 'Go on, Jessie! Don't stop!' Then the doorbell pealed, followed by a louder crash, and Meggy-Mony-Feet vanished on her treacly feet.

I sat bold upright and realized the whole house was shivering and shaking, so I hastily put on my dressing-gown and slid down the banisters to find what was afoot. Bush did not come out of the kitchen to meet me as he normally did but lay whimpering in a corner with his paws covering his ears. I could hear thumps and thuds from outside: dustbins rattling, slates skidding off the roof and the garage door creaking as it swung to and fro. And the doorbell ring-ring-ringing . . .

A louder crash roused H.J. from his slumbers and he came sleepily out of his bedroom to hang over the banister and call down, 'Is something happening?'

'Yes! Come down!'

It did not take him long to assess the situation. 'I'd better go out and see about that garage door,' he said, shrugging on a waterproof over his pyjamas. 'Help! I can't get the door open.'

Suddenly it flew open of its own volition and out he went in a headlong rush, never to come back. Had he been blown into the next parish? I was too busy running backwards and forwards, rescuing rugs and kitchen utensils to bother about him, distracted all the time by that persistent ringing at the front doorbell. I was not sure if someone was trying to get in or if the noise was caused by the gale.

At last I tugged the door open and Miss Calder tumbled in. She fell headlong into my arms in a great state of distress, gasping out a terrible tale that her precious pug-dog was lost.

'Blown away!' she wailed like a banshee.

Even on her best days I thought Miss Calder looked like a witch, with her hunched back, crooked teeth and straggly hair. Tonight I would not have been surprised to see her mounted on a broomstick. 'It's all right,' I said soothingly and conducted her to a chair in the hall. 'Sit there! I'll find your wee dog.' It was just something to say.

A crash from the kitchen and H.J., looking almost as wild as Miss Calder, came clattering back. He held something in his arms.

Miss Calder rushed at him and snatched her precious pug. 'My pet! Thank goodness you're safe!' H.J. looked startled for a moment, fearing she was about to embrace *him*, but she was too busy cuddling her smelly dog; so we abandoned her and tried to cope with the next emergency.

It was all like a nightmare, yet exhilarating. No sooner had we dealt with one problem than another arose, so there was no time to feel sorry for ourselves. At one point, a large pane from the study window blew in, showering us all with shoals of sharp glass. The telephone wires, of course, were blown down, leaving us completely cut off; the garage door *did* fly off its hinges, the clothes from our washing-line were whipped away, and Granny – one of our chimney-pots – came toppling down with an almighty crash.

And still the innocent missionary slept peacefully through it all and knew nothing about it till we told him while he was eating his boiled egg in the morning.

There were others worse off than ourselves. During the height of the storm a man stumbled into the kitchen with blood streaming from his brow. He was a tramp, I discovered later, who had been hit by a flying slate. I sat him down, and, after patching him up, managed to produce a pot of tea.

We were all drinking the brew when Mr Sturrock came running through the hall. I had never seen him move so swiftly before, but it was the force of the gale which had propelled him along the passage. 'Dreadful, isn't it?' he gasped, holding on to the kitchen table. 'Anything I can do to help?'

'No thanks, Mr Sturrock. Have a cup of tea.'

On such a night we were all kin.

The storm settled down as all breezes do, but it left the parish plenty to talk about and provided H.J. with a powerful sermon: God moves in a mysterious way His wonders to perform. It was 'our gale' and we were proud to see it mentioned in the local newspaper. There was even a photograph of debris scattered across the road – not, thankfully, the Manse washing – and I made a wee story out of it about Meggy-Mony-Feet being saved because of her treacly tootsies. And so it was all grist to the mill, as Jessie would have said.

The gale hastened another stormy period at the Manse: the spring-cleaning.

Fain would I have ignored it had I not been constantly pestered by folk asking, 'Have you started yet?' *They* had started early because of the patching-up that had to be done in the aftermath of the gale.

It was the chief topic with the local wives who made a fetish of turning their houses tapsulteerie (upside-down) each spring till they had extracted every vestige of dust from beneath their beds, killed every cobweb from the corners, beaten the life out of their carpets and exhausted themselves in the process.

Their disconsolate husbands could be seen mooching about like knotless threads. 'There's nae place to sit doon,' they complained glumly. Sometimes they, too, would be forced to roll up their sleeves, paper the parlour, beat the rugs, hang curtains and mend cupboards till their houses were spick and span. Thereafter they were ordered to wipe their feet outside the door and take off their boots before venturing into a newly cleaned room. It was a period of purgatory for them.

And for me.

No one could boast of more dust under the beds than I could. (*Oose* Jessie called the dust.) Or more painting and patching needed than in the Manse; but I could easily turn a blind eye to such deficiencies. Quite easily! Mrs Sturrock, of course, was the first to finish.

'I'm through!' she told me triumphantly. 'You must come and see the spare bedroom. It's got new paper with wee sprigs of roses on it, and new curtains to match. It looks a treat. When are you beginning?'

'Oh! soon!'

I thought about it every day but somehow could not find the impetus to make a move. At one point, in desperation, I took down a picture in the drawing-room, but when I saw the mark it left I hastily put it back again and abandoned the whole operation.

Meantime, old Miss Calder was calling for help, and it was while I was beating her carpets hung over the clothes-line that I decided I might as well use my energies on the Manse dirt.

'Yes! I've started!' I told Mrs Sturrock; though the truth was I had only turned out a kitchen drawer and discovered so many lost treasures ('So *that's* where my thimble is, and here's the minister's fountain-pen!') that it took ages to sort everything out, and more ages to shove them back again, higgledy-piggledy. After which the drawer was untidier than ever and I couldn't find a thing. But at least I had started.

I was quite good at climbing the step-ladder, but once up was not sure what to do except come down again. It was Oor Net who suggested employing her father as handyman.

'He's no' doing naething, an' he can turn his hand to onything.'

Any port in a storm. Hogg was risky but cheap. He always began a job slowly and deteriorated as he went along, stopping at frequent intervals to wipe his moustache and complain, 'I'm dry!'

The only brew I could offer was tea which he drank in great gulps while sitting on the stairs looking as if he had just moved mountains. Before long both he and I were covered with Manse dirt, so at least some of it had got shifted, and with whitewash from the morning-room ceiling. I had decided to tackle it first as it was the smallest room, the one nearest the door, into which visitors could be shown to await the minister's pleasure. There was nothing much in it except a table and some chairs, but it seemed as big as Buckingham Palace by the time Hogg had splashed his way around it.

The trouble was, he was not as steady on the step-ladder as I was. 'Canny stand heights! Look oot! It's shooglin'.' So I had to prop up the ladder and dodge the splashes of whitewash that dropped down on my nose.

I was a bonnie sight when the doorbell rang and I discovered Aileen on the doorstep with Jasper at her heels. 'Can you come for a walk?' she began, then took one horrified look at me. 'What on earth are you doing?'

'Spring-cleaning,' I said sadly.

'Poor soul!' She shook her head and turned away. It was all beyond her comprehension.

By the end of the day Oor Net and I had washed and ironed the curtains, and by dint of much coaxing and multiple cups of tea induced Hogg to re-hang them. He was no handier with a hammer than a paint-brush, and both of us were sporting blood-stained bandages on our thumbs before the deed was done.

But the room was clean. And I was so proud of it I did not bother to clean myself but kept opening the door and keeking in to admire my handiwork.

'Isn't it nice?' I said to H.J. when he came home. He had sensibly banished himself all day from the scene of battle. 'Don't you think we've made a good job of it?'

Alas! He scarcely noticed it, not that there was much to notice, but marched straight into his un-spring-cleaned study, calling over his shoulder, 'What's for supper?'

8. No Place Like Home

'Have you ever thought of running away?' I asked Wee Wullie one morning.

I was really asking the kitchen sink, since I was there at the time, and so was Wee Wullie, hanging about waiting for the minister to give him a fiddle lesson.

Wee Wullie was my anchor, ready and willing to run errands, take the puppy for a walk, shoo the pet lamb out of the door, pump up water, and *listen* to me even when I was only talking to myself. Unlike the rest of the Hogg family who were constantly gabbling, he had the precious gift of silence, so we got on a treat.

'Were ye thinkin' aboot it?' he asked me presently.

'What? Running away?'

I wrung out the dishcloth as if screwing someone's neck. Yes! I thought about it many a time, visualizing the thrill of walking out of the door with not a care in the world and just wandering away on my own. Forget about minding my p's and q's! To hell with the washing-up and the minister's meals! Damn Mrs Sturrock and the Woman's Guild!

Usually I got rid of my spleen at the sink or by plying the pump at a furious rate; but on one occasion I did run out of the Manse in a fit of black despair and marched up the road, not knowing where I was going. And not realizing Baa-Baa was following me till I almost bumped into the Pisky Parson.

'Hullo!' He gave me a quizzical glance. '*You*'re in a hurry!'

'Oh hullo!' I said sheepishly. (Well, lambishly, I suppose.) 'I'm just – er – taking Baa-Baa for a walk.'

'Well, you've got a nice day for it,' he said with a smile; this was not strictly true, for it was smirring with rain at the time. 'What about coming in for a cup of tea?'

This was the first invitation I had received from the Episcopalian preacher. I realized we were outside his gate and that I knew nothing of his private life or what went on behind his curtains. Indeed, I knew little about him at all, and our occasional encounters always seemed to take place in unfortunate circumstances. But this was not the time to delve deeper.

'No thanks!' I said hastily. 'It's time I was getting back to make the minister's supper.'

As I turned and fled with Baa-Baa at my heels, the black dog on my back had vanished; but goodness knows what the Pisky Parson thought of me. Oh well! it didn't matter.

'It was the gypsies,' I said to Wee Wullie, remembering what had brought on today's fit of longing for freedom. 'I see they're camping in the Loaning.'

They had looked so free and untrammelled seated round their open fire that I envied their raggle-taggle way of life. Out in the open all day long; no responsibilities; come and go as they pleased. True, the women were toothless, their faces browned by the wind and the wood-smoke, the men's hair was matted, the lean dogs fought, and the children chewed sticks of rhubarb with no sugar to sweeten the sourness. But they were *free* and seemed contented enough with the lot they had chosen.

'I seen them,' said Wee Wullie.

He spoke quietly, even for him. Was something bothering him? Perhaps he was weary of waiting for his music lesson.

'The minister won't be long,' I consoled him. 'Would you like me to go and hurry him up?'

'No! dinna!' said Wee Wullie urgently.

I looked at him more closely. Surely these were not tears in his eyes! Wee Wullie would never cry like a bairn.

'What's wrong, Wullie?'

He wiped his eyes and then made a confession. '*He*'s no' pleased with me.'

That surprised me. Wee Wullie and the minister always appeared to be getting on so well. The small boy looked on my brother as God. One word from Him and Wee Wullie ran to do His bidding, falling over himself in his eagerness. The minister, too, seemed to enjoy his young pupil's company and not only during the fiddle lessons. His Reverence was a great sports' fanatic and often, when he was jumping about in the garden, I noticed that Wee Wullie was there emulating him. The results were noticeable for, under God's tuition, the small boy's stunted form was filling out and he could now proudly display his biceps.

But young folk easily change their minds. 'Why is he not pleased with you, Wullie? Are you getting fed up with the fiddle?' I asked sympathetically.

'No, I'm not!' he said fiercely.

'Then what?'

Wee Wullie suddenly hit out at the sink and knocked over the porridge pan. 'Damn!'

'Wullie!' I said reprovingly. 'That's a bad word.' (Which I used myself time and again, though I tried to keep it under my breath.) 'Tell me what's wrong.'

Wee Wullie took another swipe at the sink and then burst out, 'I canna read the music notes!'

He wiped his eyes. No! He wasn't weeping though his eyes were watering. I had a sudden thought. The wee laddie was needing spectacles.

'I'll see the District Nurse,' I said, 'and she'll know what to do.'

'What aboot?' enquired Wee Wullie. He was brightening up, for he had heard the study door opening and would have been off like a shot had I not restrained him.

'Wait, Wullie! I just want a word with the minister.'

As a result of our confab a strange sight could be seen a few weeks later – Wee Wullie blinking like an owl through his new spectacles. It took ages for him to get used to them. All the Hoggs wanted to try them on, even the baby; but eventually Wee Wullie mastered them and they became part of his personality.

At first he was careful to take them off when turning cartwheels or about to embark on a fight, and his constant cry was, 'Watch ma specs!'

But the great thing was he could *see*. His music improved and he was no longer down in the doldrums. He and H.J. played endless 'duets' together; and Oor Net, listening at the study door, said proudly, 'I think Wee Wullie's *better* than the minister!'

But spectacles could not cure my own doldrums on the few occasions when the black dog settled on my back. Usually the depression was brought on by some unexpected reminder of home.

'There's a man roarin' at the front door,' Oor Net said to me one day, scuttling back to the kitchen with a scared expression on her face after answering the doorbell.

'What's he roaring about?'

'I dinna ken. He's no' speaking *words*. I'm feart!'

So I went, and saw a familiar figure on the doorstep – a regular visitor to the farmhouse at home. It was Yorkie the tramp, bawling for sustenance and swiping at the rhododendron bushes with his walking-stick. Ordinary tramps came to the back door, but Yorkie was not a 'proper' vagrant. It was said he came from a good family and had become a wanderer after his mind was deranged. My father knew how to deal with him and could always calm him down. I was not sure if I could do the same, but I could try.

'Sit down,' I said, pointing to the steps leading up

to the door. 'I'll bring you some food.'

He stopped roaring and meekly sat down, mumbling to himself, while I hurried back to the kitchen, brewed tea and cut bread-and-cheese sandwiches. Nettie meanwhile was trembling in a corner as if she was about to have her throat cut.

'He's harmless,' I assured her. 'He just makes a lot of noise.'

True! He had begun to bawl again by the time I carried out the food. I hoped no one else would call at the front door and get a wallop from his stick; but he quietened down while he munched his meal. Then he stuffed the left-overs in his pocket and went off without a backward glance.

That was Yorkie! He came and went without any explanation. But his sudden appearance at the Manse made me turn my thoughts longingly to the days when I, too, was as free as Yorkie to come and go.

So my heart leapt up when H.J. said suddenly, 'Let's go home.'

'Oh yes!'

This happened out of the blue every now and then, usually when the minister had something special to recount to Mother. And this time he had! The Moderator's visit and *his* visit to the General Assembly. She and Father would want to hear chapter and verse, and my brother liked nothing better than being the centre of his parents' attention.

Good for him! I didn't care what the reason was, as long as we went.

I was ready in two toots, waiting anxiously to see if the 'baby' would start. I crossed my fingers and held my breath till the car began to judder into life.

Hurry up before it stalls! Let's get going!

We set off in a flurry, hooting Mrs Sturrock out of the way and missing the Pisky Parson by a whisker. What did another startled glance matter? Goodbye, Mrs What's-Your-Name! Ta-ta, Mr Thing! We were on the road home.

H.J. and I sat silently side by side, thinking our own thoughts, but inside myself I was singing daft songs:

> Tam, Tam, the Gundy Man,
> Washed his face in the frying-pan.
> Kaimed his hair
> Wi' the leg o' a chair.
> Tam, Tam, the Gundy Man.

I changed tunes and tempo now and again, singing faster to help the 'baby' on its way:

> Matthew, Mark, Luke, John.
> Haud the cuddy till I get on.

When we saw our first sight of the hills H.J. changed gears and began to whistle a secular tune which sounded like 'Pop Goes the Weasel'. As I watched the scenery become more and more home-like a hundred childhood memories went whirling through my mind: eating a sugar-piece, helping to dress tattie-bogles, watching Jock-the-herd mending a drystane-dyke, hearing Jessie's stories as she milked the cows in the byre.

Would she be putting the kettle on? Try as I would, I could not visualize any feature of her face. Everything was a blur but, as soon as I saw her, it would sharpen into focus. I began to feel solemn and repeated to myself a verse Auld Baldy-Heid had taught us at the village school:

> This is my country,
> The land that begat me.
> These windy spaces
> Are surely my own,
> And those who here toil
> In the sweat of their faces
> Are flesh of my flesh
> And bone of my bone.

Hoots, lassie, stop being so sentimental! H.J. was muttering 'Damn!' beneath his breath as a pheasant ran splay-footed across the road, but I could not reprove him as I had Wee Wullie. Hurry up! We'll soon see the first glimpse of the farmhouse.

Jessie was at the door scattering a plateful of leftovers to the cocks and hens. How could I have forgotten that familiar figure? The moment I saw her I knew! Steel-grey hair firmly swept back into a bun, long black skirt, white apron, clogs on her feet, a wee shawl round her shoulders and that uncompromising expression on her face.

Maybe her back was a little more bent and, like Wee Wullie, she was wearing spectacles. I knew those communal specs which her brother Jock-the-herd shared with Jessie and her sister Joo-anne. They had slipped down her nose and she peered over them at me but did not change her expression. If she was pleased to see me, she did not show it.

I had to curb my desire to rush forward and hug her. Jessie did not hold with emotion.

'Hullo, Jessie! It's great to see you.'

'Huh! Ye're bigger, lassie.'

'Am I, Jessie?' It was always something.

I got a peck from Mother and a grunt from Father before we went into the parlour with Sonny. I scarcely listened to what the others were saying, eager for the time when I could escape to the kitchen.

'How did your hat look?' Mother asked me.

'Oh, fine!'

As usual they gave me up as a bad job and concentrated on Sonny who had plenty to say for himself. I doubt if they noticed when I edged to the door and tiptoed out of the room.

In the kitchen I could be myself. I perched on the table and made Jessie sit down in the rocker. 'Haud on! I canna sit doon when there's work to be done,' she protested.

'You can so! Come on, Jessie; tell me everything.'

But first she shut the back-kitchen door so that Phemie, the current servant-lassie who was rattling the pots and pans, could not hear.

'That article!' she complained. 'She's got lugs as big as cabbages.' (Later I had a word with the 'article' herself. She was no better and no worse than the others who had passed through Jessie's hands during the years.)

'What would you do if Phemie was perfect?' I asked Jessie, wickedly.

She shook her head. Jessie could not envisage such a phenomenon, and doubtless would have been disappointed if she could not rage at somebody. I was far from perfect myself in her sight, but I did not mind her scolding me. It was great not to be deferred to as the Lady of the Manse.

'Keep your shouthers straight, wumman!' she admonished me.

Her own 'shouthers' *were* a little more stooped.
'How are you, Jessie?'

'Howts, I'm fine!' Then she admitted, rubbing
her knees. 'Stiff!'

That was as much as she would say about herself.

I let down my hair and began to blether about all
that was happening in the parish. At least, some of
the things. Now and then I drew back, realizing
Jessie would not understand all the nuances; but I felt
I was important to somebody as she listened and
nodded her wise old powe.

As I talked I looked around the kitchen at all the
familiar objects of my childhood: the rag rug in front
of the fire where Blackie the cat snuggled, the bins
that held sacks of flour and meal, the corner cupboard (the *press*), the giant dishes on the dresser, the
mangle, the jail-stool shoved under the table; no or-
naments on the wall except the sheep-dip calendar
with its current picture of *The Fighting Téméraire*.

Memories came flooding back and I visualized the
days when the long jail-stool was brought into use at
clipping-time and I helped Jessie fetch and carry as
she fed the shearers crowding round the table. I
could smell the savoury food, hear the clatter of
plates and cutlery, the loud guffaws of laughter from
the men, and their thanks to Jessie as they finally rose
to resume their work.

'That was a guid tightener, Jessie!' Sometimes a
Geordie accent was heard from a shepherd from
over the Border who had come to help Jock-the-
herd. Fancy him calling Jessie *hinny!*

Today I could smell the same savoury aroma for,
as we talked, Jessie was keeping her eagle eye on the
pots and pans at the side of the range. Sometimes she

lifted a lid and prodded at the contents. 'That poul-
tice!' she grunted, and called to the back-kitchen.
'Phemie, did ye pit saut in the tatties?' 'Ay, I did,
Jessie!'

Jock-the-herd must have killed a sheep, for a roast
was sizzling in the oven; and no doubt Mother had
made one of her trifles – Sonny's favourite dessert –
which would be cooling in the milk-house. There
would be no 'drink' with the meal, apart from jugs
of water and milk, unless Mother had made as a
special treat a lemony concoction called Boston
cream with whole eggs-in-their-shells floating on
top till they disappeared mysteriously into the deli-
cious brew.

I licked my lips in anticipation. It was all so lavish
after the frugal fare at the Manse; but it was food for
thought that nourished me as I talked to Jessie and
listened to her pithy comments.

I think – maybe – she missed me, for she would
never 'speak' to Phemie, only rage; and I was dis-
tressed to hear her knees creak as she got up to open
the oven door. 'I'm failin',' she confessed.

Oh Jessie, dinna fail, I thought in a panic. You've
never failed me yet. I couldn't do without you.

Then suddenly she reverted to normal as I tried to
help her. 'Here! get oot ma road, wumman!' she said
in her customary cross voice, pushing me aside.
'Awa' ootbye an' get some fresh air to tak' that
peelly-wally look off your face.'

Outside I did a hop-skip-and-jump, not caring if
my stockings were wrinkled or my hair tousled.
H.J., too, having ended his session in the parlour,
came running out in his old shorts and ragged jersey.
It was good to hear him whistling and see him leap-

91

ing about like a leprechaun, no longer the minister,
just a red-haired laddie.

We all need an outlet.

I went into the field called the *cow-gang*. All our
fields had names and this one was so-called because
the cows went there. Daisy-Bell and Maggie paid no
attention to me, but I was glad to see Jock-the-herd
coming my way.

'Hullo, Jock!' I called to him.

When we met he leaned on his crook and said:
'Man-lassie!'

Jock was as uncommunicative as a drystane-dyke.

I could get more information from a conversa-
tion-lozenge, but he did give me a look and eventually remarked, 'Ay! ye're gettin' on.' I interpreted
this as meaning I was growing up. Och! but I didn't
want to be any bigger or wiser. I didn't want *anything* to change. I had a closer look at him, the same
as I had looked at Jessie. Oh Jock! *you*'re not failing,
too!

He was certainly leaning more heavily on his
crook and his old eyes were watering, like Wee
Wullie's. It was time Jessie gave him back his specs.

'How are the sheep?' I asked.

'No' bad.'

'Oh, that's good.' I looked at the dogs lying pant-
ing at his feet. 'And Jed and Jess?'

'Failin'.'

That word again! A sudden stab at my heart.
Make the most of it, I warned myself, in case it slips
through your fingers. Stop peering into the future;
take what you can *now*.

So, at the end of our 'conversation', I cried,
'Come on, Jock, give me a swing,' and ran off to the

big tree where he had built the swing for me. Would
he come? Yes! And with a sprightlier step.

It was like old times with Jock grunting as he
heaved me higher and higher till I could see over the
roof of the farmhouse. If only Mrs Sturrock could
see me now with my skirt above my knees and my
hair streaming in the wind! 'Higher, Jock, higher! I
want to see the Eildons.'

We went away with a supply of fresh eggs and
butter, as well as a basketful of apples and vegetables; and Mother admonished me as she always did
to remember who I was. (A 'lady', she meant.) A
last wave to Jessie at the door. She didn't wave back
but shook her apron at me. Down the road past the
cottages. Mrs Thing and Mrs Thingummy came out
to wave. Turn the corner and we were on the main
road. It was over!

H.J. was silent on the way back, getting himself
into gear for the more sombre duties that awaited
him. He muttered 'Silly idiot!' now and again to the
'baby' as he rattled round corners.

'Sit up straight!' I told myself as we neared the
Manse. 'You're back on duty.'

Miss Calder was on the doorstep looking for us.

'Where have you been?' she said huffily. 'I want to
borrow some desiccated coconut.'

'Oh yes, Miss Calder. I'll see if I've got some. It's
nice to be back.'

So it was – in a way.

9. A 'Fate' Accompli

Give praise where it is due, I must record that the fête was my idea though I don't begrudge God the credit for blessing us with such a sunny day.

The brainwave bounced into my head – perhaps to relieve the boredom – one day when the Major's wife was showing me round her garden at the Knowe. Mrs Major was obsessed with her garden. She had the greenest fingers and the reddest roses in the county, and her running commentaries went trickling on like a never-ending flow of water from a brook. Today, she was indulging herself, for it did not matter to her that it was *me*, just someone to admire the perfection of her purlieus.

I was fed up. It was a penance to follow her up each pathway, to linger at every plant and hear chapter and verse of their past history and future prospects. Mrs Major had their Latin names off pat, and when she was in full flood the brook became a waterfall. There was no stopping her, God wot!

I could see Leckie, who helped with the rough work, lurking at the compost-heap, hoping he wouldn't be noticed, but ready to touch his cap if she confronted him. He never saluted me when he came to do the Manse garden, just leaned more heavily on the wheelbarrow and grunted, 'Soor!', meaning the Manse soil was sour.

Not Mrs Major's. For years the Knowe soil had been treated with every conceivable form of extra to sweeten it, and wilting plants were dosed regularly with tonics to encourage growth; they also received brisk words from the Major's wife.

'Come along now! Perk up! You can do better than that!' No sensible flower would dare droop in her presence.

But I did.

I could see Leckie loping off to take refuge in one of the greenhouses. I wished I could join him or escape indoors to listen to the Major playing his pianola; but I dutifully trailed behind her, murmuring appropriate remarks. 'Lovely! Oh yes, very nice!' hoping she wasn't pointing out a nettle.

Then out of the blue I heard myself making a heartfelt statement, 'It's really beautiful!'

It had suddenly struck me that the garden *was* lovesome. I had never looked at it properly before, only at Mrs Major's behind as I stepped after her, but now I gazed around me and realized it *was* worth ad-

95

miring. The combined efforts of Leckie, the house-guests who were dragooned into helping, the Major when he couldn't escape, and, of course, Herself at the helm, had resulted in a veritable riot of colour and fragrance. Bees were buzzing dizzily among the honeysuckle, butterflies fluttered towards the candytuft, the roses were bursting into full bloom and the close-cropped lawns were spick and span. Not a weed in sight; it was all perfect.

I began to feel giddy myself with all the mingled perfume. Otherwise I would never have had the audacity to say, 'What a pity folk can't see it!'

Mrs Major turned round and gave me a surprised look.

'What do you mean?'

'Well . . . er . . .'

What *did* I mean? I had to say something. And having put my foot on the trough, I plunged right in. Splash!

'I mean everybody,' I said recklessly. 'All the parishioners. They've heard so much about your garden but never seen it. What a treat it would be for them if you could throw the garden open and hold a fête.'

I knew I had gone too far and was horrified at my impudence. So was the Major's wife. She drew herself up to her full imposing stature and let out what could only be called a snort.

'In my garden! What utter nonsense! Plenty of people see it. All my visitors . . .' She stopped and looked around her as I had done, then she said in a contemplative way, 'In a week or two it will be really perfect. I suppose we *could* erect a marquee on the lawn. But it would need a lot of thought. A lot of thought!' She twirled the trowel in her hand. 'A fête, did you say . . .?'

'I could speak to my brother,' I said hastily and, while she was pondering, took the opportunity to steal away, wishing I had bitten out my tongue.

But the deed was done and there was no going back.

'A good idea!' said H.J. when the news was broken to him. He accepted it as his own and set about organizing the event with his usual zeal. In any case, he was better equipped for the job than I was and, being on such genial terms with the Major, he helped to clinch matters with Herself who soon stopped wavering and began to think it was *her* idea.

The news spread like wildfire. 'A FATE!' said the parishioners when they heard of it. It was a new word to them, except to Mrs Sturrock who declared that of course she knew; she had been to hundreds in her day. ('Name one!' I was longing to ask.) Oh yes! She knew all about Fates. 'You walk about the garden and then you get your tea.'

'Right!' I said, seizing the opportunity. 'Will you be in charge of the teas, Mrs Sturrock?'

Yes, she would. She'd be delighted! It would mean hob-nobbing with the gentry. She would get the Woman's Guild to help; and, as for me, it was one problem solved. I was learning the art of delegating instead of rushing at everything myself.

We had to persuade some of the Doubting Thomases that a fête would be fun. The Thomasinas were more easily won over. It would be a thrill to be a guest in the gentry's garden instead of peering through the gate as they sometimes did on their evening strolls. And think of the excitement of dressing up for the part!

The men were more reluctant to put on their Sunday best merely to stroll through a well-kept garden. What would they *do*? H.J. soon inspired them with his enthusiasm and by conjuring up suggestions for activities to keep them occupied. There would be an entrance-fee at the big gates for the Schemes of the Church (that pleased Mr Sturrock, the treasurer); a few quiet games could be arranged – not too boisterous in such surroundings – clock-golf, perhaps, or guessing the names of the flowers and plants in the hot-houses. (I suggested Hunt the Weed, a variation of Hunt the Thimble!)

They might even try guessing the names of the guests. There were sure to be some nobs from London present.

'Holy Moses! There might even be *royalty*!' gulped Oor Net, starry-eyed. 'I'd better look oot a hat. Will I need to wear a veil?'

'You'd be as well to wear something,' I told her; and a veil would at least help to obscure her full-moon face.

There was a great washing, ironing and rummaging in wardrobes before the big day, even visits to Berwick to purchase new outfits. Help! I thought guiltily, what have I started? But it was all out of my hands by now. H.J. was at the Knowe morning, noon and night, so I kept away as much as I could, fearing Mrs Major's wrath. Though any time I went with an offer of help, she brushed me aside. 'Don't bother me! I'm busy!' I could see she was enjoying being up to High Doh; and she could let off steam to 'poor Dolly', the inoffensive relative who kept in the background, ran the house and was accustomed to being a whipping-boy.

The best I could do was make sympathetic sounds to poor Dolly who smiled bravely back and uttered not a word of complaint. The Major seemed to have grown smaller and quieter as his wife grew bigger and noisier; he played his pianola as pianissimo as possible till she raged, 'Stop that din! We must have some *real* music at the fête.'

I thought of suggesting Wee Wullie and his fiddle, but Mrs Major had the Berwick Brass Band in her sights. She could put them in one of the conservatories as long as they were careful not to blow the blooms off her precious pot-plants. 'And you, Dolly, can take them cups of tea when they have an interval . . . Now, let me see, what next . . .?'

It was all taking shape and there was no denying the garden *was* looking perfect.

'All we need now is a good day,' sighed Mrs Major, extracting a final weed from one of the borders. She straightened her back and looked skyward. 'We must pray for one.'

'I'll speak to my brother,' I murmured. *He* would be the best person to have a word with God.

H.J. must have done his job well, for the great day dawned bright and clear with sunshine floodlighting the garden. All the flowers opened out and basked in its beams. Every prospect pleased and no man was vile. Not even Mr Sturrock, who conjured up a smile as he sat at a wee table at the big gates ready to charge sixpence for the Schemes of the Church.

The parishioners queued up in neat lines, listening to the discreetly-hidden band, and speaking in hushed whispers as they craned their necks to have a first peep at the garden and at the few house-guests who were already strolling about on the lawn.

'Who's that?' The women nudged each other. 'Oh! See her with the parasol. D'you think it's Lady Somebody?'

They were not interested in the flowers, just the people.

When they surged in they did not know what to do, walk to the marquee to have tea, wander up and down the paths, or just saunter about, hoping some of the gentry would speak to them. Mrs Major was buzzing about like a giant bumble-bee. I stood behind her, acting as lady-in-waiting and trying to tell her who everyone was.

'That's Mr Scott; he's an elder. Miss Pryde who serves in the store. Baxter the policeman. Mr Thing who lives somewhere-or-other . . .'

For a time Mrs Major shook their hands affably. 'Oh! good afternoon, Mr Scott. Lovely day, Miss Pryde. Yes, the garden *is* looking lovely. Hullo, Mr er . . . er . . .'

Soon her patience was exhausted and she stopped listening to my whispered promptings. 'Just make yourselves at home,' she said, waving her hands expansively. 'I'm off to have a cup of tea.'

The parasol lady came up to me and said condescendingly, 'How d'you do? I come from London. I must say, it's very pleasant here. Don't you think so?' She held out a languid hand.

'Never mind me!' I said hastily. 'Let me introduce you to . . .' I looked around and saw Mrs Hogg – Oor Net's mother – hovering hopefully in the background. 'Mrs Hogg!' I called her forward. 'This lady has come from London specially to meet you.'

Mrs Hogg bobbed a delighted curtsey and pumped the languid hand up and down while I beat a quick retreat.

I could see Leckie, spruce in his Sunday best and as proud as punch, taking charge of some of the men whom he conveyed to the kitchen-garden to expatiate on the growth of his giant cabbages and turnips. On the way he pointed out various flowers and lapsed into bungled Latin to impress his listeners. They nodded their heads gravely, awed by his superior knowledge. There was more in Leckie than met the eye!

At intervals parishioners came up to me to ask who was who.

'Is that man no' somebody in Parliament?'

'Well, he *might* be!' I had not the heart to tell them he was only somebody's chauffeur dressed up.

'And is *she* a Lady?'

'No doubt!' I said stoutly, though I had a feeling she might be a lady's-maid. The main thing was they could gaze, goggle and speculate.

I introduced as many as I could, for to shake hands with the mighty was an accolade which would send them home happy. Some even looked at the flowers and could see at a glance how superior they were.

'Ye can tell they've got a touch o' class,' declared Mrs Brown, sniffing at a scarlet rose. 'Perfeck!' She looked around and sighed, 'Ye'd never see an ordinary roddydandrum here! An' I've naethin' at hame but ma auld aspidistra.' But she took her fragrant memories with her for Mrs Major snipped off the rose specially for her, so her sighs soon gave way to smiles.

I kept myself busy carrying deck-chairs and making myself generally useful; but my best deed

101

was to rescue poor Dolly whose harassed smile was becoming more forced. I took her off to a secluded corner, made her sit down on a wicker chair and brought her a cup of tea and one of Mrs Sturrock's fairy-cakes.

'Don't worry; it's going all right,' I assured her. 'Sit still.' When I went back to retrieve the cup she had dozed off, so I tiptoed away to feed the brass band.

The brass band had been performing nobly, playing restrained – if not refained – music to suit the occasion, not blowing too hard in case they disturbed the conservatory flowers. The pot-plants were flourishing; it was the musicians who were wilting, for the heat was terrific. I could tell they were longing to take off their jackets and play in their braces, but that would never do, with Mrs Major peeping in at intervals and giving them an encouraging wave, as if conducting them. So they just had to sit there and perspire.

I fanned a few of them with a tea-towel and, after being refreshed with tea and jammy buns, they perked up and so did the music. To the surprise of the fuchsias who began to sway up and down, they started to play more lively tunes, and were giving big blows to a Harry Lauder medley when I noticed one of the elders advancing up a pathway in quick-march time and even kicking up his heels.

This was a signal for the youngsters to let off steam. It was Wee Wullie who started it by taking off his spectacles and turning a cartwheel on the lawn in full view of some of the starchiest house-guests. Mrs Major frowned her disapproval as others followed suit, but Baxter, the policeman, soon put a stop to their pranks by threatening to 'cuff their lugs' if they didn't behave themselves. So the lads marched off to the kitchen-garden to the st-rains of 'Keep Right on to the End of the Road', hoping that some apples and pears might fall into their hands.

It was as well the District Nurse had brought her wee black bag with her, for Mrs Hogg was pursued by a wasp which chased her up one path and down another till it finally caught up on her and stung her on the neb. There was a small spate of cuts and bruises, but only one black eye when someone peered too closely at a blowing-out instrument in the brass band and was rewarded by a direct hit, whether deliberate or by mischance, who could tell?

Mrs Major had thought of *everything*.

They – the band – had a welcome respite and emerged from the conservatory for a breath of air when a piper suddenly appeared in full fig. He

marched proudly round the lawn as if leading an entire platoon into battle, and we stood around admiring his hairy knees and swinging kilt. The music was so stirring that even the staidest onlooker – Mr Sturrock – could not avoid jigging on the spot; but at last the piper's wind gave out and he trailed off into the kitchen-garden where his bagpipes gave a final sad squeak, and the brass band reluctantly returned to its post.

But at long long last they played 'Auld Lang Syne' and a double-quick version of the National Anthem.

My brother stood in the centre of a circle as if about to play ring-o'-roses and thanked everyone from the Deity to Leckie. We could not be sure that God bowed, but Leckie certainly did, not once but several times. Of course, it was Mrs Major who received the greatest applause; she was so carried away that she called for her secateurs to snip off flowers to present to everyone as they left. The garden would have been completely denuded had she not pricked her thumb on a thorn and, by the time the District Nurse had bandaged it, her euphoria had left her.

The Scouts and Brownies were set to work by vigilant elders to clear up any debris from the lawn and, by the time the gates were finally closed, it was difficult to tell there had been such an invasion.

'Never again!' sighed the Major's wife, sucking her bandaged thumb and subsiding on to the drawing-room sofa. In the next breath she murmured, 'But it was a great success.' She gazed out of the window at the garden. 'I think we could have it a week later next year. It would make all the difference to my dahlias . . .'

Help! Was it set to be an annual event?

Next day it *poured* from morning till night, which somehow made the 'Fate' seem more of a success in the eyes of the parishioners.

Leckie, looking his usual scruffy self, lurked at the Manse back door and grumbled, 'I doot it's no' worth gettin' oot ma spade. I'll just get drookit, an' ye canna do muckle wi' sic a soor gairden.'

How true!

10. Harvest Thanksgiving

Of course, the minister's job was much harder than mine. His was a real job. He had been hired as God's chosen man – as well as the parishioners' – and since this was his first church he had no backlog of sermons 'at the bottom of the barrel'. So he was forced to produce two split-new ones every week, as well as children's addresses and prayers. No wonder his brow was furrowed as Sunday loomed near.

The poor soul took ages to work himself into the right mood before settling down to write a sermon. He would do anything else in the study: practise golf shots, shuffle the books on the shelves, blow dust off the mantelpiece, even lie down on the floor and do his exercises; and, of course, play the fiddle.

I knew he was looking for inspiration when I heard him pacing up and down, stopping occasionally to play a snatch of music, not really playing, only 'fiddling'. Sometimes I was tempted to poke my head round the door with a suggestion: one of Jessie's stories about the bubblyjock, for example. Surely he could find a suitable text for it in the Old Testament.

When I heard a triumphant twiddly-bit, I knew he had had a brainwave. Thereafter peace would descend as he began to scribble out his discourse in the straggly writing which only he could decipher; and I would have to keep Bush and Baa-Baa at bay for the duration.

Sometimes he had to fit his sermon to the occasion. The Harvest Thanksgiving lent itself to inevitable quotations about sowers going forth to sow, and ploughing the fields and scattering.

> Come, ye thankful people, come,
> Raise the song of Harvest-home!
> All is safely gathered in
> Ere the winter storms begin.

Leckie, the beadle, hated the Harvest Thanksgiving and grumbled about the mess to be cleared up afterwards, but at least the kirk moose would be pleased. And *I* was quite pleased, too, to see the results of my labours, for I had helped to decorate the church the day before. Mrs Sturrock had commandeered me, along with Miss Steele, the organist, and Mrs Leckie, the beadle's wife. It was a new experience for me. In the little kirk at home we had only one sheaf of corn to mark the occasion; but here they made a great to-do and everyone was involved.

Parishioners flocked to the church door bearing bunches of chrysanthemums, twigs of rowan berries, baskets of vegetables, tomatoes, loaves of bread, even a dead hen. The gentry had raided their greenhouses for exotic plants, and sent offerings of figs, grapes, peaches and plums. Far too good for the kirk moose!

Everything had to be displayed, else offence would be taken, but it was difficult to make artistic arrangements of outsized onions, turnips and potatoes. 'Just dump them on the pulpit stairs,' Mrs Sturrock suggested, 'and hope the minister doesn't trip over them.'

There was nothing comparable in the Manse garden, but I felt we had to make a contribution. 'It'll have to be eggs,' I told my brother. Our few hens were laying nice brown ones by now, so I sacrificed half-a-dozen and placed them in a wicker basket at the foot of the pulpit. Another obstacle for the minister to avoid.

When he finally picked his way up the steps he could scarcely be seen, for the pulpit was festooned with fronds of autumn leaves and corn dollies. I wondered if he was tempted to help himself from a basket of fruit placed within his reach – the ripe plums were mouth-watering – but he restrained himself and, apart from an occasional plop as some hips and haws fell their moorings or when a tomato rolled over, all was serene.

The heady aroma of fruit and flowers was so potent I almost nodded off during the long prayer. Hiding my head in my hands and sniffing the country smells, I thought back to crisp autumn days on the farm; the back-end of the year when the wild fruit on the hedgerows ripened, the rowans were bright red, and the crab-apples which we called *scrogs* were ready to eat. I used to sit up a tree sampling them, and gathered great basketfuls which Mother and Jessie made into scrog-jelly which had a sharp, bitter-sweet taste.

I recalled how we tried to hoard like the squirrels, though it was a problem knowing what to do with surplus fruit and vegetables. The men dug potato and turnip heaps, Jessie made enough jam to see us through the winter, Mother bottled plums in glass jars, and tried to preserve eggs in a sticky substance called isinglass. They never came up to the standard of fresh ones but 'kepped a catch', as Jessie said, meaning they were better than nothing when we were snowed in.

We laid eating apples out on the spare-bedroom floor, row upon row, being careful that none of them touched; but, of course, the mice soon touched them, and often we were left with nothing but the cores.

It was the corn itself that mattered most, and Father's annual revenue depended largely on garnering a good crop. To that end everyone laboured in the fields early and late, working on till the wee sma' hoors and taking advantage of God's lamplight, the full moon. I remember toddling after the carts in the eerie half-light and hearing the men raise a cheer when the last sheaf was forked from the field.

Then the cycle would start all over again. Seed-time and harvest . . .

The long prayer had come to an end and I was roused from my reverie by a buzzing sound in the kirk. It came from the direction of the organ which sometimes made strange sounds if Miss Steele pulled out the wrong stops. (Stranger if *I* was acting as her stand-in!) A bummy-bee, lured by the fragrant smells, had joined the congregation. Everyone sat up and took notice as it zoomed around Miss Steele's head, and Leckie grabbed a Bible to use as a battering-ram if it came within reach. Then the minister gave out the children's hymn – 'Day by Day the Little Daisy' – and Miss Steele was forced to begin playing.

We watched, fascinated, as the intruder settled on her hat before winging away in the direction of the pulpit. H.J. did not notice it till the hymn ended, by which time it was buzzing dizzily round his head. I had to admire the way he coped with the situation. Taking up his sermon he dealt a direct hit on the offender and the bee fell to the floor, if not dead then with a bad headache. Then H.J. calmly gave out his text: 'As ye sow, so shall ye reap.'

At the end of the service I helped to gather up the spoil and distribute it to poor or ailing parishioners. After trudging miles to reach their cottage doors, both the flowers and I were wilting, but I felt I had done *something* to earn my title of Lady of the Manse. Meantime, Leckie was busy with a big broom, sweeping away the debris; and the kirk moose, I hoped, had put on weight.

But that was not the end of the Harvest Thanksgiving.

On many farms there was a jollification to come, a Harvest Home, called in the Borders a *kirn*; a thanksgiving spree laid on by the farmers to reward their workers for the extra hours they had toiled in the fields. It was the highlight of their year, and they

worked as hard at enjoying themselves as they did when forking sheaves in the stackyard.

The kirn was held in the granary which had been cleared of its sacks, swept out and then garnished with greenery before sprinkling soap-flakes on the floor to make it slippery enough for dancing. The cobwebs hanging from the rafters added a touch of 'decoration', and the merriment lasted till dawn, with a plentiful supply of food and drink provided by the farmer. So much, indeed, that the story is told of an old shepherd being repeatedly ejected before being carried home protesting, 'I dinna care! It's been a verra dry affair, onyway.'

The kirn held on the farm at home was the first social affair I ever attended. I can vaguely recall being carried up the granary stairs and sitting half-asleep on Jessie's knee, listening to Wattie the Fiddler playing rousing reels and watching the dancers birling round in their tackety boots. The men discarded their jackets and rolled up their shirt-sleeves and the women screamed with delight when they were whirled off their feet. I could hear the horses stamping in the work-stable and the cows mooing down below in the byre. Then I drowsed off and heard nothing till I awoke in my own bed.

I had attended many a kirn since then, but none as lively as the one we – my brother and I – were invited to in the parish. It was to be held on the biggest farm in the neighbourhood, the Mains, and we were bidden to arrive at the farmhouse at seven o'clock sharp.

I liked the Meikles who lived at the Mains. Mr Meikle was an elder of the kirk, a decent salt-of-the-earth chap; his wife was a gentle self-effacing woman who never uttered a wrong word about anyone, even, I suspected, about me. She was an excellent cook and a fond mother to her family of strapping sons who would inherit their father's farm in due course.

Their sister Mary was my favourite, a fresh-faced pretty creature as gentle as her mother. I used to think of her as Sweet Mary and wondered if the minister might look in her direction when he started courting. It was only a thought. Certainly he was taking some pains to spruce himself up for the kirn, and even looking out his dancing-pumps.

'You'll get your feet trampled on,' I warned him, remembering the tackety boots at our home kirn.

'We've been invited to the house,' said H.J., brushing down his jacket. 'You never know; they might be going to hold it in the drawing-room.'

True enough, the room was enormous, and perhaps their intention was to lay down a drugget carpet and hold the festivities there. But, in the event, it was held in its customary venue, the granary, and H.J. never changed into his dancing-pumps. He would have been better with a pair of shin-guards.

The Meikles were still skedaddling to and fro when we arrived at the Mains at seven sharp. The young lads were shrugging themselves into their good jackets, while Mrs Meikle whipped off her apron and Sweet Mary tied a pink sash round her waist. Mr Meikle rolled down his sleeves and we all stood about in the hall till we heard the sound of bag-pipes outside.

'Are we all set?' asked the farmer, leading the way. The farm-manager and his wife were waiting outside and we fell into our proper places to form a procession. Mr and Mrs Meikle led the way, with the lads and Sweet Mary behind. Then came the minister and myself, with the manager and his wife bringing up the rear. The piper played louder as we marched through the yard, into the barn, and up the stairs to the granary where the assembled company awaited us. We were greeted with great cheers and applause as if we were conquering heroes returning from the wars. I had forgotten how loud a pair of horny hands could clap; it was like guns going off.

The granary had been decorated to the hilt with greenery, corn-sheaves, streamers and pot-plants. Looking around, I saw that all the Mains's workers were there and also invited guests from neighbouring farms. Some of the village folk as well, including Leckie and the Hoggs – even Henry John who could not be parted for long from his source of sustenance – and Oor Net who was a bobbydazzler, wearing what looked like a nightdress tied in the middle with bindertwine. She was sporting a pair of high-heeled shoes but I suspected she would soon be in her stocking-soles.

The Hogg baby was not the only one waiting for provender. As soon as the clapping subsided the company scrambled to their places and grabbed their knives and forks ready for action. It was a sit-down affair – a real tuck-in – with giant steak-pies, mounds of vegetables, and second helpings for everyone. There were tarts, oatcakes and cheese to follow, beer to drink for the men, and lemonade for the youngsters.

The minister said a special grace for the occasion, and they were off with a great clatter of cutlery and loud guffaws of laughter as they exchanged 'bars' between mouthfuls. (A *bar* was a daft joke, and they had all been saving up a 'stotter' for the occasion.) As the beer flowed the tongues loosened, except for the farm-manager's. His face was growing redder as the time approached for the speeches, for he knew he would have to stand up and reply to the farmer.

Mr Meikle could scarcely be heard above the cheers as he thanked the workers and hoped they would have a happy evening. No doubt about it! They sang 'For He's a Jolly Good Fellow' at full strength, and clapped fit to wake the dead.

Then, 'Come on, Geordie!' they cried encouragingly, and the manager was helped to his feet, looking as if he was about to be hung. He began to speak in a 'put on' voice, very unlike his normal one, and had frequent keeks at a tattered piece of paper from which he had been practising his speech for weeks. His wife, who was word-perfect, mouthed every syllable with him and was ready to prompt him when he lost the place. He ended in his normal voice with, 'Three cheers for the maister an' missis,' and it was over. What a relief! He sat down, had another helping of steak-pie and thought himself the hero of the evening.

There was a great clearing away of dishes and stacking up of trestle tables before the floor was swept clean and sprinkled with soap-powder. Two fiddlers perched themselves on chairs placed on top of a table and tuned their strings ready for the opening dance.

The company broke out into loud 'Hoochs!' in anticipation, but had to restrain themselves for there was a set pattern for the opening dance. The farm-manager, now elevated to M.C., announced the Circassian Circle and then invited the farmer's wife to be his partner. Meanwhile, Mr Meikle 'took up' the manager's wife, H.J. partnered Sweet Mary, and I was claimed by the oldest boy, Alastair. We had to promenade solemnly round the floor while lesser mortals made their choice and joined the parade.

Then – *thump-thump* – the fiddlers dunted their feet to show all was ready and played an opening chord. We faced our partners and bowed, the lively music began, everyone broke into unrestrained cheers – and we were off.

Thereafter there was scarcely time to breathe as one dance followed another in quick succession, all so vigorous that perspiration was soon pouring off the revellers: reels, strathspeys, the Lancers, polkas and a roundabout dance called the Hoolichan where we were passed on from one partner to another. It was a real test of stamina. Little wonder that faces grew redder, the men cast off their jackets and displayed their braces and the women blew down the necks of their dresses for coolness.

There was no ceremony in choosing a partner. The men sat on benches on one side of the room, the women opposite, and when the M.C. announced the next dance they skedaddled across the floor and grabbed a partner without a by-your-leave. There was no chance to refuse and no wallflowers left sitting on their own. Oor Net, dancing in her stocking-soles, was in the height of bliss, skirling at the pitch of her voice and doing her best to birl her partners off their feet. And often succeeding.

When a Ladies' Choice was announced the minister was swamped with would-be partners and could have danced with a dozen. I chose Leckie and waltzed round and round with him. He was great at reversing and danced with one hand behind his back in a 'gentlemanly' manner. It was the hard hands I remember most and the agility of my partners who could skip as lightly as ballet dancers in spite of their muckle boots.

Mercifully, there came a break to give the fiddlers a rest and we all sat down and breathed heavily. Cups of tea were dispensed to slake our thirst and the M.C. announced there would be 'turns' if anyone would oblige. Yes, they would! There was no shortage of offers. The trouble was to get them to stop once they started. Even the minister obliged with a song – a Harry Lauder special – 'I'm the Saftest o' the Faimly'. It went down a treat and he was cheered to the echo, but fortunately did not oblige with an encore.

Then the floor was re-swept and re-sprinkled with slippery stuff, the fiddlers wiped their moustaches and picked up their bows. Off we went again, refreshed and with fewer inhibitions than before. The stable-lamps hanging from the rafters swung to and fro, keeping time to the music, the dust rose up and danced in the air, and a few of the women began to wilt. But not Oor Net who was heard to remark, 'I'm half-deid, but I'll no' give in.' I wondered if she would be able to face the kitchen sink next day, but what did it matter? Let joy be unconfined.

I was black and blue myself by the time the Mains party took their leave. We were clapped and cheered as we left, and I had a feeling there was a sense of relief that the posh folk were departing. What happened later I can only guess, but next day Leckie had scarcely strength to lean on his spade and Oor Net had lost her voice. But a good time had been had by all, and for me it had been a welcome break in the stilted life of a Lady of the Manse.

When I went to visit the Mains a few days later to say thank you, I surprised Sweet Mary sitting in the parlour cheek-by-jowl with a young farmer who had been very attentive to her at the kirn. Her cheeks were scarlet as she jumped up to greet me and I realized I had been up a gum tree as usual, thinking she and the minister would have made a pair.

Well done, Sweet Mary, I thought. You've had a lucky escape!

11. Making a Mark

'Ye're terrible quiet,' Oor Net said to me one day while I was helping her peel potatoes at the sink.

Quiet!

The knife slipped and, as I was sucking my thumb, I wondered what she would say if she could hear me voicing my suppressed feelings. Had I given way to them, I would have been *screaming* loud enough to rouse the minister from his den. But perhaps he was sitting in the study swallowing his own emotions. We were great ones for keeping ourselves to ourselves.

'I'm just thinking,' I told Nettie, as airily as I could.

'Mighty!' Oor Net gouged the eye out of a Golden Wonder and gave me a surprised look. Silent contemplation was beyond her comprehension. Any thought that flitted into her head had to be expressed verbally before it was lost and gone for ever. 'What aboot?'

'Oh, nothing much.'

Indeed, it wasn't anything much. Just that at times I longed to throw off the Manse shackles, to run, jump, climb trees and YELL, if I felt like it. But I was learning to keep a tight rein on my emotions and to yell silently. It was the only 'sensible' thing to do.

Certainly, I did not lack exercise in the Manse, scurrying along the passages, sliding down the banisters, pumping up water and generally trying to be in several different places at the one time. That was *inside* where I seldom sat down. *Outside* I had to tighten the rein and walk sedately, reminding myself that critical eyes were watching every step.

What I dreaded was, it might become automatic. What if I grew up to be tight-lipped and disapproving, like the late minister's sister? 'Oh no, never!' I comforted myself, flinging a potato in the air and catching it as it came down. If I lived to be a hundred, my high spirits would still bubble over. There was no hope of my learning 'sense'. But it was a great strain, separating the daft lassie from the dignified lady. They were constantly getting mixed up.

Though older and wiser, I suspected my brother was tarred with the same brush. He was only a restless laddie at heart, and could not settle for long in

119

the study without picking up his fiddle or darting out into the garden for some fresh air.

Not, alas, to do anything useful with spade or trowel. He would bound round the lawn with Bush barking at his heels, leap over imaginary hurdles and hop-skip-and-jump into the borders, to the disgust of Leckie who disapproved of exercise or indeed of any violent activity.

Bush had run off with a tea-towel, and when I hurried out to retrieve it, I heard H.J. saying to Leckie, 'You should try it, man! It would brisk you up.'

'Me?' sniffed Leckie, leaning more heavily on his spade. 'Wi' ma sair back!' Far from brisking up he looked ready to collapse. 'It takes me a' ma time to carry the big Bible up the pulpit stairs.'

'See! That's what I mean,' said the minister, taking a great leap over a gooseberry bush. 'It would make you more supple . . .'

I left them to it and went indoors to pursue my own activities; but, as weeks went by, I knew something was germinating in the minister's mind. Not content with keeping his own body in good trim, he was determined to recruit the young people of the parish to follow his example. The best way to do that was to organize a Sports Day.

It was easy enough to convert *them*. Their needs had been neglected in the past by the 'auld meenister' who was more like a prophet from the Bible than a flesh-and-blood human being. His word had been law and they treated him with great respect, curbing their natural impulses in his presence. It had never entered his head that they might want to kick footballs, run races, jump hurdles and let off steam like all young things. So they rallied to the young minister with his sporting ideas.

The elders were not so ready to be off with the old and on with the new. 'Oh no!' they shook their heads disapprovingly. 'We never did *that* in the old days!' But these were new days, my brother told them. It was time to take a step forward.

All the same, he had to go cannily instead of rushing like a bull at a gate. It was the interests of the church he had at heart, he told Mr Sturrock. The youngsters could not be expected to support any of the excellent causes – the Schemes of the Church, for example – unless *their* needs were supported. They would drift away from the kirk and that would mean empty pews and empty coffers. And wasn't it the elders' duty to help the young folk achieve healthy minds in healthy bodies?

Constant water weareth away a stone.

Eventually Mr Sturrock gave his grudging approval. H.J. did not actually persuade him to put on shorts but, by dint of subtle suggestion, he cajoled the chief elder into agreeing to start the races on Sports Day. Another triumph for my brother!

Now there was nothing to stop him. He began at once to train the young lads who were as eager to follow him as if he was the Pied Piper. They did up-down exercises to tone their muscles, they practised the high jump, kicked footballs – and sometimes each other – in the Lang Field near the Manse, and were often to be seen rolling on the wet ground after a tackle.

'Mercy! that's Geordie doon!' gasped Oor Net, peering from the window one day. 'I doot he's deid.'

But the corpse rose up to limp away arm-in-arm

with his opponent, and it was plain they were all thoroughly enjoying the activity. Sometimes it was the minister who was 'doon', and thereafter there were times when he preached with a bump on his brow; but the young folk were there to listen to him. The day came when it was announced from the pulpit that a Sports Day would be held. All were welcome and a collection would be taken for the Missions Overseas.

This brought a mixed reception. 'Imagine oor meenister getting mixed up wi' such unholy capers! Kicking footballs! The auld meenister would birl in his grave.' But some said, 'High time! Let the young folk have their fling.' As usual I kept out of the controversy, just saying 'M'm!' and not taking sides.

None of the women would admit they wanted to go to the Sports, yet none of them wanted to stay away in case they missed something. So they drifted towards the Lang Field and huddled on the sidelines, trying not to look interested. Even Leckie abandoned his spade and hid in the background, but was soon pushing his way to the front to get a better view.

There were no events for females, not even an egg-and-spoon race, but I guessed my brother was hastening slowly and we might find our feet in days to come. I was used to being a sideliner though I longed to join in, but at least I could catch a ball if it came my way and throw it back with a direct aim.

It was an unladylike thing to do according to the woman who was standing beside me. 'I wouldn't have nothing to do with that dirty ball,' she said disapprovingly. In the next moment she was shouting, 'Go on, Tam! Kick it! Tuts! Silly sumph!'

Some neighbouring ministers had been induced
to come and watch – and not only watch, for H.J.
persuaded them to join in a men's race. Reluctantly
they took off their bicycle-clips, rolled up their
trouser-legs and set off in their stocking-soles
puffing like grampuses. The spectators were as-
tounded at such flippancy, especially when they saw
the Reverend Kennedy's big toe sticking out of his
undarned sock.

My brother ran with them, slowing his pace to let
them pass, but, when the local butcher put on speed,
pride got the better of him and he sprinted on to win.
Even Leckie joined the congregation in cheering
him, and the other ministers mopped their brows.
'Never again!' they gasped. But who knew? Perhaps
in days to come they might follow my brother's
example and organize Sports Days in their own
parishes.

So, though H.J. could not go too fast too soon, he
was at least setting a pattern for more enlightened
days to come. *He* would leave his mark on the community. There was little *I* could do but be a shadow.

I knew my duty was to back up the minister, do as
I was told and get by each day as best I could. If I felt
the stirrings of a revolt I was much too young and
inexperienced to do anything about it, so what else
could I do but stifle my feelings and do my shouting
silently?

It was left to Mrs Kennedy – Rita, the minister's
wife who lived near Berwick – to strike a blow for
the Manse ladies. The *girls*, she called them. Imagine! They were all as old as the hills in my sight.

The brethren met and conferred at intervals, she
reminded us. Why shouldn't the 'girls' follow their

example and meet in each others' Manses. They could lay on a special tea and take turns to read a paper.

This foxed me. I had visions of the ladies solemnly reading out items from the *Scotsman* or the *Berwickshire Advertiser*, but in the event it was nothing like that. The other 'girls' rallied round out of curiosity and the opening meeting was held in Mrs Kennedy's house.

I went by bus with Mrs Purves and joined the others who were sitting in a circle in Rita's drawing-room. She had dressed for the occasion in flowing robes and a hat with a little veil. She had a pile of books on a table in front of her.

'Where's the tea?' mouthed Mrs Purves, but Rita's mind was above food.

She took up one of the books and began to read poetry to us in such mellifluous tones it was difficult not to be lulled into a dreamlike state. I did not really listen to the poetry but watched the changing expressions on her face; dreamy one moment, sad the next, then as happy as if she had captured a sunbeam. It was fascinating.

Some of the 'girls' nodded off, but who could blame them? They were unaccustomed to sitting still in a warm room with nothing to do. Mrs Purves had such a guilt complex that she had brought her knitting with her and purled and plained mechanically while stifling her yawns

We were all in a soporific state – except the speaker – when her crumpled husband poked his head round the door and hissed, 'Rita! The tea!'

The ladies sat up and shook themselves awake. 'Tea?' said Rita in a faraway voice. 'Oh yes! It's all ready next door, I think.

We all trooped next door before she could embark on another poem and found that, indeed, the table had been laid though in a somewhat higgledy-piggledy fashion. There was an artistic arrangement of flowers in the centre and a few plates of buns and sandwiches spread around, but it was not a *spread* in the sense of a good tuck-in tea. Still, it was better than nothing and, when Mr Kennedy brought in the teapot, tongues were loosened and the ladies chit-chatted animatedly about home affairs.

Not one of them mentioned 'the reading' so I felt impelled to go to Rita who was sitting gazing into space with that elevated look still on her face. 'That was nice,' I said inadequately and then struggled for something else to say. 'It must be wonderful to be so fond of poetry . . .'

'Oh, it is!' agreed Mrs Kennedy, trying to focus her gaze on me. 'It takes you out of yourself.'

Good for you, I thought! Rita had found *her* escape-route.

Though the other ladies were not similarly inspired, they liked the idea of getting away from their humdrum routine so they agreed to take turns in their Manses and vied with each other to lay on a good tea. The only drawback was that dreadful 'paper'.

We would all have got on fine if we had just gossiped; but it was Rita's idea and she insisted the object of the meetings was 'culture'. So the ladies made brave efforts to produce something to make the others think. Some read deadly dull essays which I suspected their husbands had supplied – miniature sermons, they were – and others gabbled a chapter from any-old-book, the faster the better, for we were seldom listening, just wondering what kind of tea would follow.

My turn did not come for ages but, when it did, I puzzled over the tea rather than the reading and decided to make it as dainty as possible to suit Rita. She was still Mrs Kennedy to me but I felt we had something in common, being both inclined to be otherworldly. So I spent ages making tiny sandwiches and cutting off the crusts (though I saved *them* for future use), baked wee buns with icing on top, and a gingerbread that fell in the middle.

I tried to cover up my deficiencies – and follow Rita's example – by making an artistic decoration in the centre of the table with bronze leaves.

'It's not bad,' conceded Oor Net when I was putting the finishing touches to the table. 'What will ye speak aboot?'

'Oh dear, I can't think! Have you any ideas, Nettie?'

'God!' said Oor Net. I was not sure if she was swearing or answering my question. '*He* always gangs doon well.'

'Oh no! I couldn't talk about *Him!*'

'What aboot Moses?' suggested Wee Wullie who had brought in the branches of bronze leaves.

But I rejected Moses, too, and was still undecided when the ladies assembled upstairs in the drawing-room. Rita took a seat at the window and gazed at our untidy garden as if that was enough for her. I knew they did not expect much from me but my hackles rose when one of the older wives smiled patronizingly and said, 'Don't worry, my dear. We'll let *you* off.'

I was not going to be treated like a child. I would say something, no matter what. Help me, Jessie! Suddenly I thought of the happy times I had spent with her in the byre when she was milking the cows.

'I'll tell you a story,' I announced, to the company's surprise, and embarked on the one about the scarecrow (only Jessie called it the *tattie-bogle*) and the turkey-cock (which she called the *bubblyjock*). Having started, I had to go on, and gradually I forgot to feel self-conscious. I just went on till the story was finished.

The tale had a meaning, I suppose, something like a parable, though Jessie never made a point of it and I had never noticed it in the old days. But the ladies seemed to like it and gave me a little round of applause.

'Tell us another,' begged Mrs Purves who had put away her knitting.

'Oh no! The tea's ready.'

I felt that neither the tea nor my contribution to culture had been substantial enough, but at least my turn was over and it would be a long time before it came round again.

Rita, looking dreamy as usual, was nibbling at an

egg sandwich. She spoke to me in a low voice, 'I feel quite inspired.'

'Oh good!' I said, looking at the bronze leaves. 'I hoped you would like them.'

She had not even noticed them. 'No, no! I mean your story.'

Mercy me! I must remember to tell Jessie next time I went home. She would be pleased. It was basically *her* story though I had toshed it up a bit.

But Rita wasn't finished with me. 'Why aren't you writing down your stories?' she wanted to know.

(For the same reason that you're not writing poetry, I wanted to tell her. When can a Manse mouse find *time*?)

'Oh, I'll keep on trying,' I said, pressing her to another sandwich.

Maybe I *could* make my mark, after all.

So I kept on trying and was taken aback when the Pisky Parson stopped me in the street one day and asked, 'What were you up to last night?'

'Last night?' I said guiltily. I racked my brains but could not recall any misdemeanours.

'In the wee small hours!' he reminded me. 'I had to go out and see a sick parishioner and noticed your bedroom light was still on.'

'Oh! was it?' The Pisky Parson always caught me on the wrong foot, so I tried to dodge past him and said airily, 'Maybe I just forgot to switch it off.'

And maybe I didn't! I wasn't going to tell *him* about my midnight escapades.

Truth to tell, the greatest boon about living in the Manse was the electric light. I never got over the thrill of pressing a switch and – hey presto! – the whole world was lit up. No tedious filling of lamps with paraffin, no polishing the fragile 'chimneys' which so easily broke in the hand, no dread of running out of oil and having to resort to candles. A Fairy Queen simply waved a magic wand and said, 'Let there be light!'

We still kept oil lamps in reserve so that we could cope with power failures When this happened I felt badly done by as I blew on the glass chimneys and rubbed them carefully with a duster. It was not a task I could delegate to someone as ham-handed as Oor Net, and the minister had never polished anything in his life. So, when the 'electricity' was working full-tilt, I made good use of it.

Looking back, I can trace my chronic insomnia to the nights when I fought against sleep in order to squeeze an extra hour or two of 'leisure'. It was the only time I could steal in which to make my mark.

Once I shut my bedroom door my real life began. Sometimes I switched off the light to fool H.J., if I heard him on his way to the bathroom, and sometimes I looked longingly at the bed thinking what bliss it would be just to sink down to sleep. But I seldom gave way to such weaknesses. How could I hope to become a 'writer' if I did not seize the fleeting hour, no matter how late?

It was during those wee small hours that I began to write my first serial story to be published later in the *Weekly Scotsman* and called – strangely enough – Lady of the Manse. It was full of 'romance' which I knew little about, but it had an authentic background of Manse life; and when I read the tattered copy today the same feeling of weariness comes over me till I have to prop my eyes to keep from falling asleep.

But having drafted it out I cast it aside, thinking how could I publish *that* while being a genuine Lady of the Manse? So, remembering Rita's advice, I scribbled out some of the stories Jessie had told me and sometimes fell asleep before I could get up to turn off the light.

It seemed no time before I was sliding down the banisters to begin another busy day and, when I looked at my notebook, I often could not make head or tail of my scribbles.

I was always so preoccupied with my own secret thoughts that I did not notice real-life stories happening before my eyes.

But I was soon to wake up.

12. Happy Ending

There was no doubt the minister was a Christian. I was rapidly reaching the conclusion that I wasn't.

Not when dealing with old Miss Calder who was becoming the heaviest burden I had to bear. I had to count up to ten before answering some of her snide remarks and swallow hard to stem the expletives that rose to my lips. If I had let fly, I could easily have outdone Oor Net.

'Shut up, you interfering old baggage! Holy Moses! You're the world's worst gossip. I'm fed up with you. Fed up! FED UP!'

I thought it but never said it, of course. Instead, I gave her a wan smile and agreed with whatever she was saying. 'Yes, Miss Calder. Of course, Miss

Calder. I'll come round as soon as I can, Miss Calder, and see if I can mend your window. No! It'll be no trouble.'

Selfish old hag! What else had I to do, she assumed, but jump to her bidding? Even her thanks, when she bothered to give them, were grudging; but a true Christian would not expect gratitude. Turn the other cheek! If you're lucky, you'll get a good mark in the Golden Book.

Some day, I promised myself, I really would turn and rend her. Watch out, Miss Calder!

H.J. was much nicer to her, though for all I knew he, too, was swallowing some sizzling words. In any case, Miss Calder's approach to him was different. While she used *me* as a kind of whipping-boy to get rid of her spleen, she was as sweet as pie when speaking to the minister, though all the time trying to Nosey-Parker some information out of him.

He had a habit of saying 'M'm!', pretending not to understand her and changing the subject so suddenly she was forced to retreat. Or he retreated himself, saying hastily, 'Sorry, Miss Calder. Must go to a meeting. I'm late!'

I had no such excuse. She would follow me even into the kitchen and stand over me while she delivered her sideways blows.

Go away! Can't you see I'm up to the elbows in flour! You'll spoil my shortbread, you silly old sow! I'm NOT going to listen to you!

But I did. I was duty-bound to be 'nice' to everybody, even Miss Calder.

One day she pursued me all the way upstairs to the spare room where I was preparing the bed for a visitor. I was not sure who it would be, but H.J. told me he would soon be expecting one and I must try to make the room as bright as possible. So I was struggling with the giant sheets and pillow-cases when Miss Calder, let in by Nettie, loomed in the doorway.

I stifled a 'Damn!' under my breath and said hastily, 'Oh, not now, Miss Calder. I'm too busy.'

But Miss Calder was not too busy. She glanced inquisitively around the room and asked, 'Are you expecting a visitor?'

'No,' I answered truthfully. Then, seeing her look of disbelief, I added weakly, 'It's the minister's guest.'

'Ah!' said Miss Calder triumphantly. 'Who is it?'

I shook my head. 'Don't know. It could be a missionary. Or maybe the Moderator,' I said wildly.

Miss Calder shook *her* head, dismissing missionaries and Moderators. Then suddenly she faced me and demanded, 'Tell me! Do you know what your brother's up to?'

'Up to?' I said hopefully. I wondered if she was going to tell me H.J. had taken up burglary as a hobby. 'He's away at a meeting.'

'He goes to a lot of meetings, doesn't he?' she said with a crooked smile.

'Well, it's his job, Miss Calder,' I said with a touch of sharpness in my voice. And none of your business!

'Oh!' she said mysteriously. Then, seeing there was nothing more to be winkled out of me, she turned away, leaving me to my bed-making.

Good riddance! I thumped a pillow as if I was pummelling Miss Calder and soon forgot about her as I went about my daily duties.

All the same, I remembered to take a quick look at H.J. that evening when he came back from his meeting, to see if there were any signs of his nefarious goings-on. No! He was the same as usual except that his meeting must have gone well, for he was whistling, and for once his first request wasn't, 'What's for supper?' Instead, he took up his fiddle and began to play in quick-time.

Good! This might be the opportunity for me to run out and meet Aileen for one of our snatched encounters. I was eager to tell her about the letter I had received that morning from the BBC. It was a secret that had been burning in my breast all day. I could pop the sausages in the oven and they would be ready by the time I ran back.

'I won't be long,' I promised H.J., popping my head round the study door.

'Oh!' he said in an abstracted voice. 'Take your time.' No doubt he wanted to go over a tricky piece of music without being disturbed. That suited me fine.

I sped along the side road leading to the big houses. Bush darted after me, stopping now and again to ferret for rabbits in the ditch. Would Aileen be there? Yes! I could see her leaning against a gate to regain her breath with Jasper tugging impatiently at the lead. Aileen's walks were always punctuated with stops and starts; both of us were out of breath by the time we came face to face.

'Oh hullo!' we said simultaneously, pleased to see each other.

'How are things?' I asked, taking her arm and helping her along the road. I was longing to tell her

my news, but I curbed myself to listen to her story first.

Aileen shied from discussing her writing with her indulgent parents who did not take it seriously – it was only a 'nice hobby' for their frail daughter – but I knew it was much more than that; she had been bottling up something to tell me.

Her eyes were sparkling as she spoke. 'D'you know what? I did a whole page of the book today. That's why I'm so tired.'

'A whole page!'

For a moment I forgot my own story for this indeed was surprising news. Usually Aileen gave up after the first few sentences, lacking the drive or the strength to press on. Sometimes it seemed as if her pen was too heavy to hold and, though she had all day in which to write, the incentive was not there.

This was *my* self-imposed task, to provide the impetus and urge her on.

So I cried out, genuinely pleased, 'Good for you, Aileen! You must press on!'

'Yes, I will!' she resolved. 'If I do a page a day I might *really* finish it.'

I wondered? She was talking of 'Nelly' her book about Nell Gwyn. I doubted if she and Nelly would ever reach the winning-post together. But in the event, thank goodness, I was to be proved wrong. She did make it; and had I foreseen the future I would have been pleased to know her publisher – John Long – was part of the firm, Hutchinson, my own eventual publisher. But that was far away in the mists of years to come.

Tonight it was enough to know she was working happily on her 'hobby' and was lively enough to discuss it with me. But it had taken its toll. 'I'm exhausted,' she said suddenly, and leaned more heavily against me. 'I had better go home.'

I walked to the gate with her, slowing my pace to suit hers. The lights in the dining-room were on, and I could see one of the maids, in neat cap and apron, moving around a table gleaming with silver. Then she drew the curtains.

'Help!' I cried guiltily. 'The minister's sausages! They'll be burnt to a frazzle!'

As I opened the gate for her Aileen said, 'Wait! What about your news?'

'Oh! it's nothing much,' I said hastily. 'The BBC wants me to broadcast one of my stories.'

'What?' Aileen clung to the gate for support. 'But that's wonderful news! Tell me more.'

'Can't! The sausages!' I said breathlessly. 'I'll try

to see you tomorrow.'

As I ran back to the Manse at full speed I bumped into the Colonel and almost knocked him flat. 'Oh, I say!' he protested. 'Steady on, boy!' But I had no time to stop and apologize.

I was conscious of someone peering through the hedge as I rushed up the garden path: Miss Calder, no doubt, on the look-out to see if a missionary or a Moderator would arrive.

But nobody came that night and nothing unusual happened. Except that, though the sausages *were* burnt, H.J. didn't utter one word of complaint.

Next morning my eyes were opened.

Spring was in the air and so was romance. Especially in the kitchen where Oor Net was mooning over the sink with a wet dishcloth in her fist. At intervals she sighed gustily as she gazed into space; and when Nettie sighed it was a full-blown blast.

'Wouldn't you like to go out and play?' I suggested, thinking she might be feeling caged as I often was myself.

In the school playground across the way the girls were skipping merrily through a long rope to the tune of 'One-two-three-a-leerie', but Oor Net showed no inclination to join them. I doubt if she even noticed them; she was too busy sighing and clutching the wet dishcloth to her bosom.

Then, suddenly, she caught sight of someone striding into the playground and her whole attitude changed. He was a lad I knew vaguely as Eck, an overgrown youth with long arms, breeks too short for him, and a fine crop of blackheads on his face. Not a heart-throb in any way. But love is blind, and obviously Eck was an Adonis to Oor Net.

She gave a little squeal, flung down the dishcloth and was off like a shot.

'Oh!' I retrieved the dishcloth and continued Nettie's work. 'So that's it!' Now and again I glanced through the window to watch the progress of their romance.

Was it romance? There were no visible signs of affection between them, quite the opposite. They hit out at each other as they chased around the playground. Eck grabbed a handful of Nettie's hair, she twisted his nose, then they both screamed as if they were being murdered.

At one point Oor Net fell flat on the ground and Eck began to belabour her with his fists. It looked so deadly I wondered if I should rush out to her aid. Then I told myself, 'Don't be daft! It's all part of the love-game. Leave the young things alone.'

I felt as old as the hills.

Oor Net was black and blue when she came back, but her eyes were sparkling and she sang lustily, 'One-two-three-a-leerie' as she grabbed the dishcloth. I could see she was not in the kitchen but away up on a rosy cloud.

I wished it was happening to me.

There appeared to be an epidemic in the air. The twittering birds were serenading each other as they fluttered about, building their nests. The doves were cooing lovingly to each other, and even Bush had a hangdog look about him.

Mercy! Was it catching, like the measles?

It was Leckie, of all people, who opened my eyes. Usually he just grunted at me as he leaned on his spade, but today he stood up straight and asked me a question:

'Have you met her yet?'

'Who?' I asked innocently.

'Hoots! The minister's intended. I hear he's coortin'.'

'Coortin'?' Good gracious! That meant courting. So *that* was what H.J. was up to!

At last the light began to dawn. Miss Calder's pryings, the mysterious visitor, my brother's mild behaviour last night – it all added up. Something had happened, something I had been too blind to see.

Certainly, I had vaguely noticed H.J. playing softer music of late. Was that a sign? And, certainly, he had been not only absent-minded but absent of body a great deal. Not just 'away at a meeting' but away in Edinburgh. On duty or pleasure?

It was pleasure. Still waters run deep.

Holy Moses!

He did not tell *me*, of course, but had written a letter to Mother, so it all came out. Before long a photograph of his 'intended' appeared on the study mantelpiece. And there she was, the future Lady of the Manse. She looked nice, serene, sensible; much better suited to run a Manse than I was. And H.J. had a look of smug contentment about him.

So that was it!

Was I pleased? My first reaction was to jump in the air and shout, 'Hooray! I'm free!' But I had become accustomed to curbing my feelings. Hold on! I told myself. Behave properly!

I congratulated H.J. warmly, admired the photograph, then walked down the village street to buy him a special treat for his supper – and for his intended who was coming to spend the night.

Walked! I could scarcely keep my feet from *danc-*

ing. I jiggled with the basket by throwing it into the air and catching it as it came down, then I kicked a stone along the street in front of me. Why not? It wouldn't matter now if I jumped over the hedge.

But, steady on! I was not free yet. Mrs Sturrock was looming towards me.

'*You*'re looking very bright this morning.'

'Yes! It's a lovely day.'

'It's drizzling,' she said disapprovingly, and gave me a sharp look as she passed by. Never mind! I would soon be out of her thrall and the Lady on the mantelpiece could cope with her tantrums.

I called in at Sarah Googly's sweet-shop to buy some peppermints for the minister. *She* was in a bright mood, but she always was, in spite of her pains. It was then I realized how much I would miss her and many of my friends in the parish; but surely I could come back and visit them as an ordinary human being?

As she twisted a paper poke for the peppermints she looked at my flushed face and remarked, 'Aye! I wouldn't be surprised if ye soon get a lad.'

'Me?'

I shook my head vigorously and went out chewing a sweetie.

No! No more entanglements for me. I had been hedged in for long enough. Just let me escape to lead my own life!

I thought of that letter I had received asking me to go to the BBC studios in Edinburgh to broadcast one of my stories. Help! Could I do it! Yes! The back's made for the burden. As one door closes another opens.

I did not feel the weight of my heavy shopping-basket as I made my way back to the Manse. I was doing a hop–skip–and–jump when I was aware of the Pisky Parson watching me with an amused smile on his lips.

Smile away! I thought, giving another little hop. I'm not a Lady any longer.

I'm myself!